As a devotee of renowned quilt designer *Pat Sloan*, you have cause to celebrate — here's the collection you've been waiting for! We've hand-picked eleven of Pat's all-time favorite designs, published in McCall's quilt magazines, and tucked them conveniently into one handy leaflet. The best of the best is now at your fingertips!

From the spring-fresh florals of *Mint Tulips* to *Trumpet Blooms* with its quick-and-easy fusible web and machine appliqué, these beauties evoke the charm and whimsy that are trademarks of Pat's appealing designs. These folksy quilts are fun to create and a pleasure to exhibit on a wall or draped atop a bed. They're sure to be cherished family favorites!

LEISURE ARTS, INC.
Little Rock, Arkansas

TABLE *of* CONTENTS

MEET *Pat Sloan*

For designer Pat Sloan, quilting has "shaped up" into an occupation she never would have dreamed of pursuing.

Although Pat grew up sewing and crafting (she jokes that she's sewn "since I could find a needle in the house"), she didn't start quilting until a friend persuaded her to take a class ten years ago. Since then, quilting has become Pat's favorite activity.

This enthusiasm for quilting led Pat to quit her job as a human resources specialist a few years ago. Her experience teaching quilting classes and creating models for a local quilt shop convinced her that she wanted to spend her time quilting. Designing was almost an afterthought. "I just had to find a way to quilt full-time," Pat says.

Her style tends toward old-fashioned, yet whimsical, quilts and wall hangings — not surprising, since she finds much of her inspiration in old Baltimore Album appliqué quilts, which she feels have "lots of personality." Pat's designs are also inspired by the simple style of the Amish. Although she spent most of her childhood in New Jersey, Germany, and Belgium, Pat often visited relatives who lived near Amish Country in Pennsylvania. She loved the distinct Pennsylvania Dutch art as a child and has seen its influence in her own unique style.

And Pat's quilting style has caught on, leading her to establish Pat Sloan & Co., which designs and publishes patterns for quilts, penny rugs, and rug hooking. Recently, Pat added fabric design to her list of accomplishments. She even has a dedicated family of quilting fans who are sometimes referred to as "Sloanies." When asked to what she attributes her success, Pat responds, "I believed I could do it … I enjoy what I do, and hopefully other people will enjoy it, too."

Quiet TIME

Finished Size: *43" x 57" (109 x 145 cm)*

FABRIC REQUIREMENTS
Yardage is based on 45/44" (109/112 cm) wide fabric.

⅞ yd (80 cm) **total** of assorted pastel prints
2⅞ yds (2.6 m) of green dot
⅜ yd (34 cm) of green print
⅜ yd (34 cm) **total** of assorted medium
  pink prints
¼ yd (23 cm) of cream print
⅜ yd (34 cm) of binding fabric
3⅝ yds (3.3 m) of backing fabric

You will also need:

51" x 65" (130 x 165 cm) rectangle of batting

CUTTING OUT THE PIECES
*Refer to **Rotary Cutting**, page 64, to cut fabrics. All measurements include a ¼" seam allowance. Borders are cut 4" longer than needed for "insurance" and will be trimmed to correct size after measuring quilt top center. Refer to **Needleturn Appliqué**, page 67, to use patterns, page 7.*

From assorted pastel prints:
- Cut 60 rectangles 2½" x 6½".

From green dot:
- Cut 2 *lengthwise* strips 4½" x 40½".
- Cut 2 *lengthwise* top/bottom borders 8½" x 30½".
- Cut 2 *lengthwise* side borders 8½" x 60½".

From green print:
- Cut 18 leaves (**A**). Cut 18 leaves reversed (**Ar**).

From assorted medium pink prints:
- Cut 18 flowers (**B**).

From cream print:
- Cut 18 flower centers (**C**).

From binding fabric:
- Cut 6 binding strips 1¾" wide.

ASSEMBLING THE QUILT TOP
*Use a ¼" seam allowance and refer to **Piecing and Pressing**, page 65, and **Assembly Diagram**, page 6, to assemble the Quilt Top. Refer to **Needleturn Appliqué**, page 67, for appliqué technique.*

1. Matching right sides and long edges, sew 20 pastel print rectangles together to make a **Row**. Make 3 Rows.
2. Sew 3 Rows and 2 green dot strips together as shown to make **Quilt Top Center**.
3. Fold each border in half crosswise and lengthwise; finger press folds. Unfold borders and use pressed lines as placement guides. Appliqué leaves, flowers, then flower centers to borders, leaving at least a 3" space between appliqués and short raw edges of border.
4. Follow **Adding Squared Borders**, page 71, to sew top/bottom borders, then side borders to Quilt Top Center to complete the **Quilt Top**.

"This was the first 'strippy' setting I designed, and I've loved this setting ever since! It's a great way to use up scraps in the pieced strips. I added lots of simple flowers to the border, and I use this quilt in my home when spring first arrives." — Pat

FINISHING

1. Follow **Quilting**, page 72, to mark, layer and quilt as desired. Our quilt is machine outline quilted around the appliqués. The flower centers are quilted in the ditch. The borders have a vine and leaf design and the rows have a continuous wavy line.

2. Follow **Making A Hanging Sleeve**, page 75, to make and then attach a hanging sleeve, if desired.

3. Follow **Binding**, page 76, to sew binding to quilt top using desired method.

Assembly Diagram

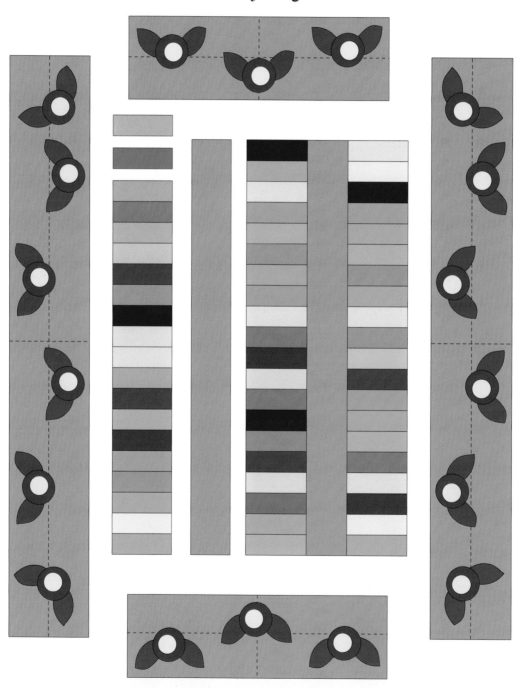

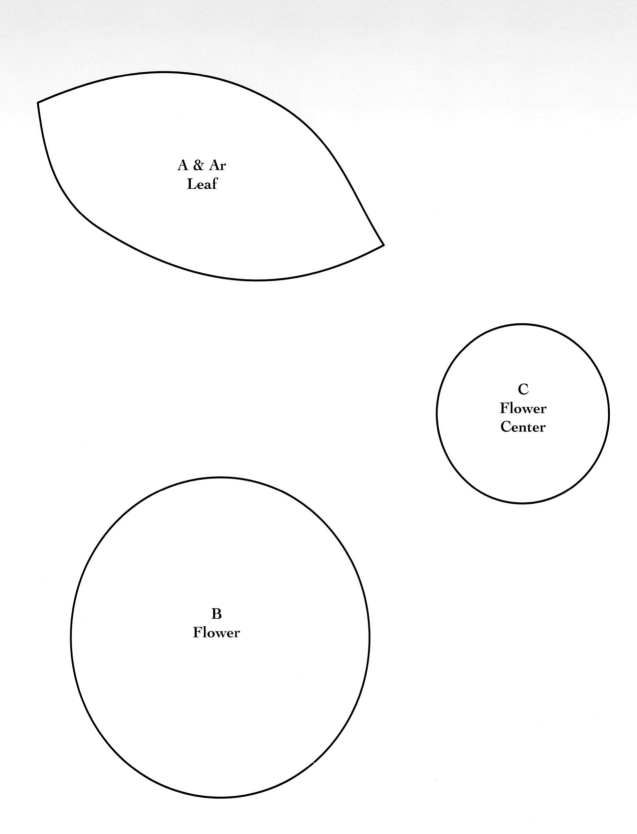

A & Ar
Leaf

C
Flower
Center

B
Flower

Pat's PERENNIAL

Finished Size: 20" x 27" (51 x 69 cm)

FABRIC REQUIREMENTS

Yardage is based on 43/44" (109/112 cm) wide fabric.

- 8½" x 12" (22 x 30 cm) rectangle **each** of cream prints No. 1 and No. 2
- ¼ yd (23 cm) of cream print No. 3
- 10" x 12" (25 x 30 cm) rectangle of lavender stripe
- ⅜ yd (34 cm) of burgundy print No. 1
- 6" x 6" (15 x 15 cm) square of burgundy print No. 2
- ¼ yd (23 cm) of burgundy solid
- 7" x 12" (18 x 30 cm) rectangle of blue stripe
- 8" x 12" (20 x 30 cm) rectangle of blue print
- 7" x 14" (18 x 36 cm) rectangle of green print
- ⅛ yd (11 cm) of light green print
- 4" x 4" (10 x 10 cm) square **each** of 3 assorted purple prints
- 6" x 6" (15 x 15 cm) square of gold print
- ⅞ yd (80 cm) of backing fabric

You will also need:

- Paper-backed fusible web
- 24" x 31" (61 x 79 cm) rectangle of batting
- Stabilizer (optional)

CUTTING OUT THE PIECES

*Refer to **Rotary Cutting**, page 64, to cut fabrics. All measurements include a ¼" seam allowance. Borders are cut 4" longer than needed for "insurance" and will be trimmed to correct size after measuring quilt top center. Refer to **Preparing Fusible Appliqués**, page 68, to use patterns, pages 12-13, and to cut stem **A**.*

From cream prints No. 1 and No. 2:
- Cut 1 rectangle 6½" x 10" (**No. 1**).

From cream print No. 3:
- Cut 2 rectangles 6½" x 10" (**No. 1**).

From lavender stripe:
- Cut 2 inner border strips 1¼" x 10" (**No. 2**).
- Cut 2 inner border strips 1¼" x 7¼" (**No. 3**).
- Cut 2 flower buds (**D**).

From burgundy print No. 1:
- Cut 2 side outer borders 3¼" x 25".
- Cut 2 top/bottom outer borders 3¼" x 18".

From burgundy print No. 2:
- Cut 4 stars (**I**).

"When my first fabric line was introduced (Old Blooms from Pe3B Textiles), I wanted to make a small wall hanging to try it out. While selecting final pieces for the line, we had 3 small pieces to work with. This quilt was made from those small pieces, which is why the background has 3 different fabrics." — Pat

From burgundy solid:
- Cut 3 binding strips $1^{3}/4"$ wide.

From blue stripe:
- Cut 2 inner border strips $1^{1}/4" \times 10"$ (**No. 4**).
- Cut 2 inner border strips $1^{1}/4" \times 7^{1}/4"$ (**No. 5**).

From blue print:
- Cut 4 corner squares $3^{1}/4" \times 3^{1}/4"$.
- Cut 1 vase (**C**).

From green print:
- Cut 1 center stem $^{3}/4" \times 11"$ (**A**).
- Cut 2 stems (**B**). Cut 2 stems in reverse (**Br**).
- Cut 2 calyxes (**E**).

From light green print:
- Cut 21 leaves (**H**).

From assorted purple prints:
- Cut 3 flowers (**F**).

From gold print:
- Cut 3 flower centers (**G**).

ASSEMBLING THE QUILT TOP

*Use a $^{1}/4"$ seam allowance and refer to **Piecing and Pressing**, page 65, and **Assembly Diagram** to assemble the Quilt Top.*

1. Sew 4 cream No. 1 rectangles together to make **Quilt Top Center**.
2. Matching short edges, sew 1 No. 2 and 1 No. 4 inner border strips together to make **Side Inner Border**. Make 2 Side Inner Borders.
3. Matching short edges, sew 1 No. 3 and 1 No. 5 inner border strips together to make **Top/Bottom Inner Border**. Make 2 Top/Bottom Inner Borders.
4. Sew Side, then Top/Bottom Inner Borders to **Quilt Top Center**.
5. Referring to **Adding Borders with Corner Squares**, page 72, sew outer borders and corner squares to Quilt Top Center to complete piecing the **Quilt Top**.

ADDING THE APPLIQUÉ

*Refer to **Quilt Top Diagram**, page 11, and photo, page 8, for appliqué placement. Refer to **Blanket Stitch Appliqué**, page 69, for technique.*

1. Working in alphabetical order, arrange appliqués on Quilt Top; fuse in place.
2. Blanket Stitch around appliqués to complete **Quilt Top**.

FINISHING

1. Follow **Quilting**, page 72, to mark, layer and quilt as desired. Our quilt is machine outline quilted around the appliqués and outer borders. There are bubbles quilted in the background and a repeating leaf pattern in the outer borders.
2. Follow **Making A Hanging Sleeve**, page 75, to make and then attach a hanging sleeve, if desired.
3. Follow **Binding**, page 76, to sew binding to quilt top using desired method.

Assembly Diagram

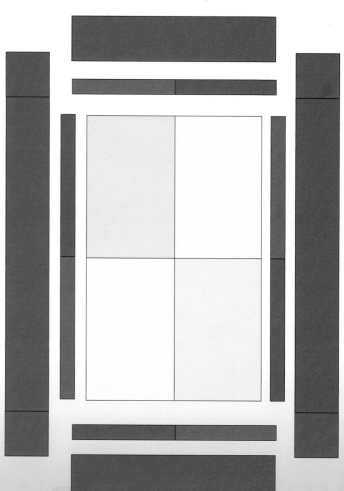

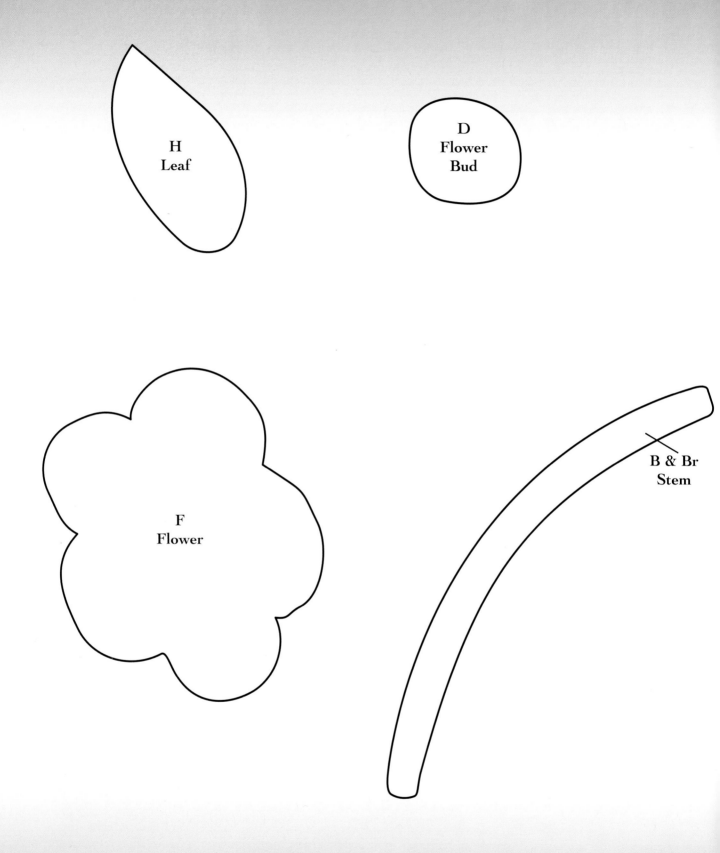

H
Leaf

D
Flower
Bud

F
Flower

B & Br
Stem

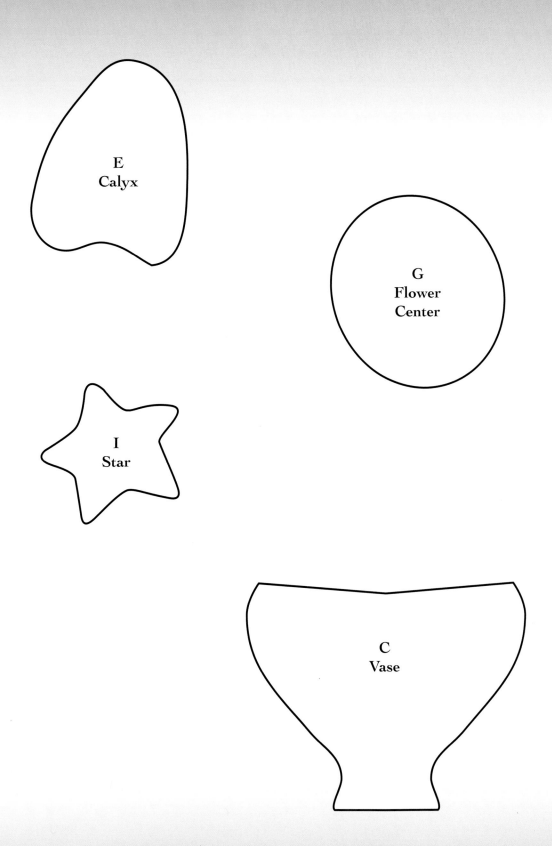

E
Calyx

G
Flower
Center

I
Star

C
Vase

Star CRAZY

Finished Size: 67" x 67" (170 x 170 cm)
Finished Block Size: 16" x 16" (41 x 41 cm)

FABRIC REQUIREMENTS

Yardage is based on 43/44" (109/112 cm) wide fabric.
Note: Except for tan print, all fabrics shown are flannel.

    $2^7/8$ yds (2.6 cm) of tan print
    $3/8$ yd (34 cm) of multi-color check
    $1/4$ yd (23 cm) of purple print
    $1^1/4$ yds (1.1 m) of purple stripe
    $5/8$ yd (57 cm) of dark pink print
    $5/8$ yd (57 cm) of dark pink stripe
    12" x 12" (30 x 30 cm) square of pink print
    $3/8$ yd (34 cm) of neon green print
    $3/8$ yd (34 cm) of lime green print
    $1/4$ yd (23 cm) of gold print
    $1^3/4$ yds (1.6 m) of multicolor print
    $4^1/4$ yds (3.9 m) of backing fabric

You will also need:
    Paper-backed fusible web
    75" x 75" (191 x 191 cm) square of batting
    Stabilizer (optional)

CUTTING OUT THE PIECES

*Refer to **Rotary Cutting**, page 64, to cut fabrics. All measurements include a $1/4$" seam allowance. Background and corner squares are cut larger than needed and will be trimmed after appliquéing. Borders are cut 4" longer than needed for "insurance" and will be trimmed to correct size after measuring quilt top center. Refer to **Preparing Fusible Appliqués**, page 68, to use patterns, page 19.*

From tan print:
- Cut 5 strips $18^1/2$" wide. From these strips, cut 9 background squares $18^1/2$" x $18^1/2$".

From multi-color check:
- Cut 6 short sashing strips $1^1/2$" x $16^1/2$".
- Cut 2 long sashing strips $1^1/2$" x $50^1/2$", piecing as necessary.

From purple print:
- Cut 20 wreath sections (**A**).

"This quilt was a challenge. I have friends who love the color lime green and wanted me to make a lime quilt. My first effort didn't meet their expectations, so when I saw this lime fabric, I knew it was the one. I used tan background blocks, then added wreaths of purple and pink stars and a fun-and-funky lime green border. They all agreed: This was a lime quilt." — Pat

From purple stripe:
- Cut 2 *crosswise* side inner borders 1¹/₂" x 54¹/₂", piecing as necessary.
- Cut 2 *crosswise* top/bottom inner borders 1¹/₂" x 56¹/₂", piecing as necessary.
- Cut 1 strip 9¹/₂" wide. From this strip, cut 4 corner squares 9¹/₂" x 9¹/₂".
- Cut 25 stars (**B**).
- Cut 25 small ovals (**E**).

From dark pink print:
- Cut 25 wreath sections (**A**).
- Cut 7 binding strips 1³/₄" wide.

From dark pink stripe:
- Cut 20 stars (**B**).
- Cut 20 small ovals (**E**).

From pink print:
- Cut 4 stars (**B**).

From neon green print:
- Cut 20 commas (**D**).

From lime green print:
- Cut 25 commas (**D**).

From gold print:
- Cut 49 large ovals (**C**).

From multicolor print:
- Cut 4 *lengthwise* outer borders 7¹/₂" x 56¹/₂".

APPLIQUÉING THE BLOCKS

*Refer to **Block and Corner Square Diagrams** and photo, page 14, for appliqué placement. Refer to **Blanket Stitch Appliqué**, page 69, for appliqué technique.*

1. Fold each background and corner square in half lengthwise, crosswise, and diagonally; finger press folds. Unfold squares and use pressed lines as placement guides. Work in alphabetical order to arrange appliqués on background and corner squares; fuse in place.
2. Blanket Stitch around appliqués. Centering appliqués, trim **Blocks 1** and **2** to 16¹/₂" x 16¹/₂" and **Corner Square** to 7¹/₂" x 7¹/₂". Make 5 Block 1's, 4 Block 2's, and 4 Corner Squares.

Block 1 Diagram (make 5)

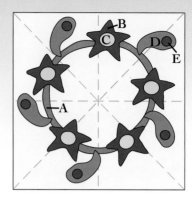

Block 2 Diagram (make 4)

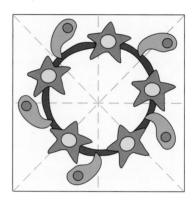

Corner Square Diagram (make 4)

ASSEMBLING THE QUILT TOP

*Use a ¹/₄" seam allowance and refer to **Piecing** and **Pressing**, page 65, and **Quilt Top Diagram**, page 18, to assemble the Quilt Top.*

1. Beginning with Block 1 and alternating blocks, sew 2 Block 1's, 1 Block 2, and 2 short sashing strips together to make **Row 1**. Make 2 Row 1's.

2. Beginning with Block 2 and alternating blocks, sew 2 Block 2's, 1 Block 1, and 2 short sashing strips together to make **Row 2**.
3. Sew Row 1's, Row 2, and 2 long sashing strips together to make **Quilt Top Center**.
4. Refer to **Adding Squared Borders**, page 71, to sew side, top, and bottom inner borders to Quilt Top Center.
5. Refer to **Adding Borders with Corner Squares**, page 72, to sew outer borders and corner squares to Quilt Top Center to complete the **Quilt Top**.

FINISHING

1. Follow **Quilting**, page 72, to mark, layer and quilt as desired. Our quilt is machine quilted in the ditch around the appliqués and inner border. Each sashing strip is quilted with a straight line through the center. There is meandering in the block backgrounds and outer border.
2. Follow **Making A Hanging Sleeve**, page 75, to make and then attach a hanging sleeve, if desired.
3. Follow **Binding**, page 76, to sew binding to quilt top using desired method.

Assembly Diagram

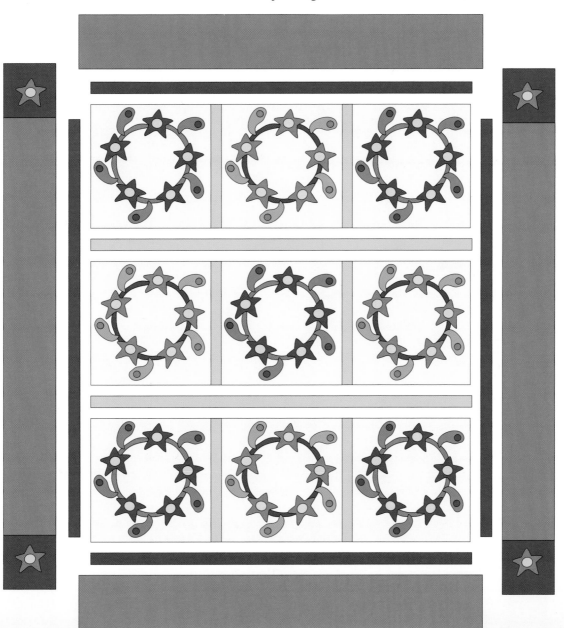

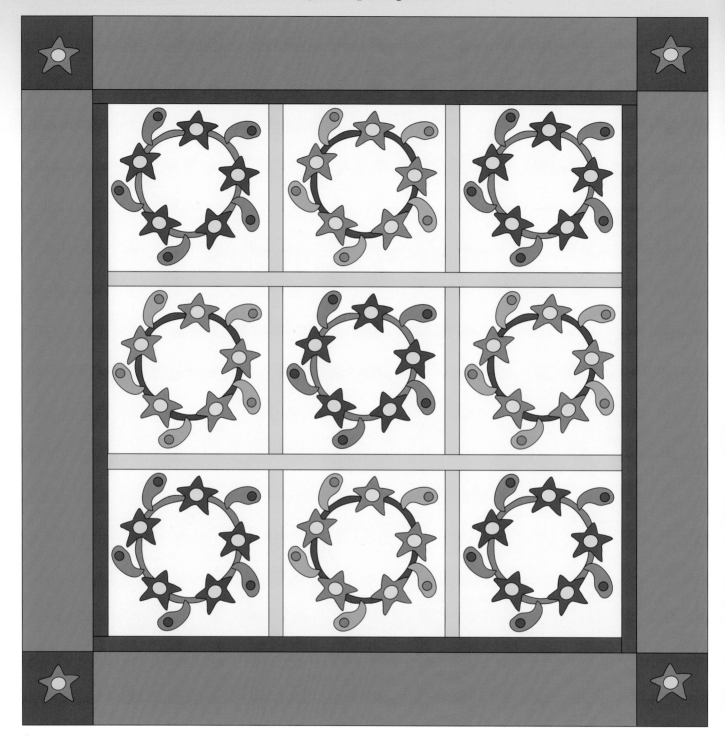

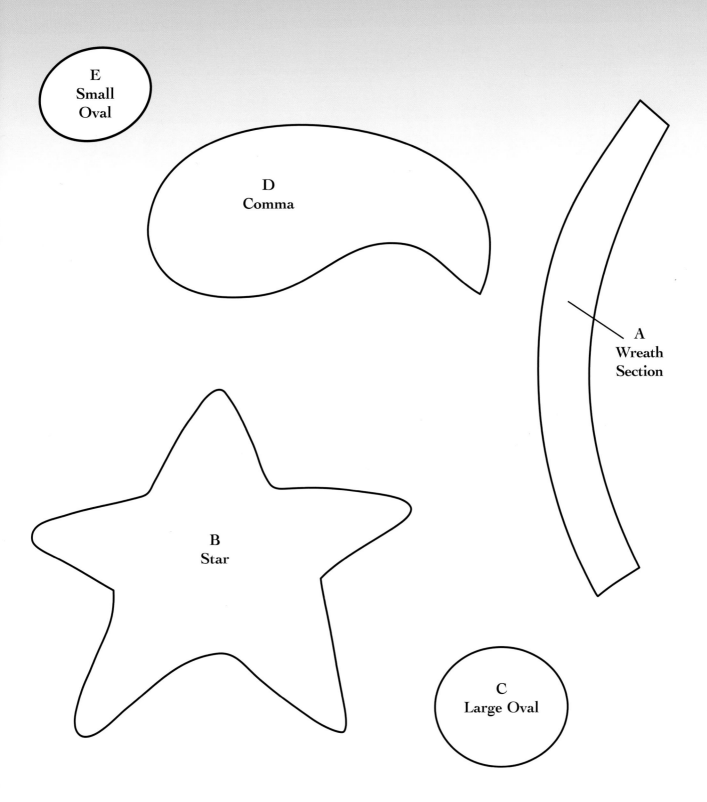

Mint TULIPS

Finished Size: 39½" x 39½" (100 x 100 cm)

FABRIC REQUIREMENTS

Yardage is based on 43/44" (109/112 cm) wide fabric.

½ yd (46 cm) **each** of 1 beige and 1 ivory print

¾ yd (69 cm) of green dot

8" x 6" (20 x 15 cm) rectangle of purple print

¼ yd (23 cm) of light pink print

⅛ yd (11 cm) of dark pink check

½ yd (46 cm) of multi-color stripe

⅝ yd (57 cm) of floral print

2½ yds (2.3 m) of backing fabric

You will also need:

Paper-backed fusible web

Water-soluble fabric basting glue

½" (12 mm) wide bias tape maker (optional)

44" x 44" (112 x 112 cm) square of batting

Stabilizer (optional)

CUTTING OUT THE PIECES

Refer to **Rotary Cutting**, *page 64, to cut fabrics. All measurements include a ¼" seam allowance. Borders are cut 4" longer than needed for "insurance" and will be trimmed to correct size after measuring quilt top center. Refer to* **Preparing Fusible Appliqués**, *page 68, to use patterns, pages 22.*

From *each* beige and ivory print:
- Cut 2 strips 7½"w. From these strips, cut 8 background squares 7½" x 7½".

From green dot:
- Cut 1 strip 5" wide. From this strip, cut 4 corner squares 5" x 5".
- Cut 1 square 16" x 16" for stems.

From purple print:
- Cut 4 flowerpots (**A**).

From light pink print:
- Cut 9 flowers (**B**).
- Cut 4 flowers (**Br**).

From dark pink check:
- Cut 3 flowers (**B**).
- Cut 4 flowers (**Br**).

From multi-color stripe:
- Cut 2 side inner border strips 1¼" x 32½".
- Cut 2 top/bottom inner border strips 1¼" x 34".
- Cut 5 binding strips 1¾" wide.

From floral print:
- Cut 4 outer border strips 5" x 34".

"In the middle of winter, I'm always ready to make a light and airy quilt, something that says 'spring' over and over! I found I was drawn to the great pink flowers in the border fabric of this quilt, and tulips are spring to me!" — Pat

ASSEMBLING THE QUILT TOP

*Use a 1/4" seam allowance and refer to **Piecing and Pressing**, page 65, and **Quilt Top Diagram**, page 23, to assemble the Quilt Top. Refer to **Blanket Stitch Appliqué**, page 69, for appliqué technique.*

1. Sew 2 beige squares and 2 ivory squares together to make **pieced square**. Make 4 pieced squares.

2. For stems, refer to **Making A Continuous Bias Strip**, page 68, to use 16" green dot square to make a bias strip 1$\frac{1}{4}$" wide x 166" long. Cut strip into four 11$\frac{1}{2}$" stems (**C**), eight 8$\frac{1}{2}$" stems (**D**), and eight 6$\frac{1}{2}$" stems (**E**). Press each long edge $\frac{1}{4}$" to the wrong side or use bias tape maker following the manufacturer's instructions.

3. Fold each pieced square in half diagonally; finger press folds. Unfold squares and use seamlines and pressed lines as placement guides. Referring to **Block Diagram** and photo, page 20, arrange 1 stem (**C**), 2 stems (**D**), 2 stems (**E**), flowerpot (**A**), and 5 flowers (**B** and **Br**) on pieced square; use basting glue to temporarily hold stems in place. Fuse appliqués in place. Blanket Stitch around appliqués to complete **Block**. Make 4 Blocks.

Block Diagram (make 4)

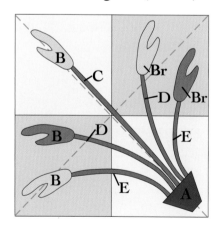

4. Sew 4 Blocks together to make **Quilt Top Center**.

5. Referring to **Adding Squared Borders**, page 71, sew inner borders to Quilt Top Center.

6. Referring to **Adding Borders with Corner Squares**, page 72, sew outer borders and corner squares to Quilt Top Center to complete the **Quilt Top**.

FINISHING

1. Follow **Quilting**, page 72, to mark, layer and quilt as desired. Our quilt is machine outline quilted around the appliqués and inner borders. There is meandering quilting in the block backgrounds and outer borders.

2. Follow **Making A Hanging Sleeve**, page 75, to make and then attach a hanging sleeve, if desired.

3. Follow **Binding**, page 76, to sew binding to quilt top using desired method.

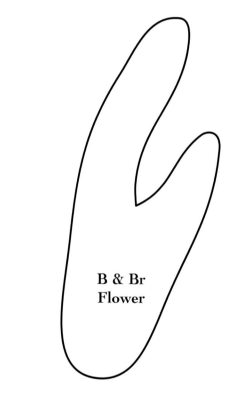

B & Br
Flower

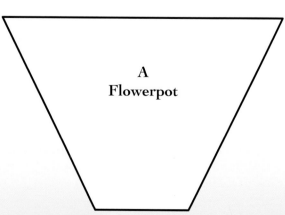

A
Flowerpot

"When selecting the fabrics for this quilt, I loved the blue and purple combination. The border appliqué repeats the leaf on the block and then I added a chain block to each corner. I'd love to see this design made up as a bed-size quilt." — Pat

Late Summer BLOOMS

Finished Size: *43" x 43" (109 x 109 cm)*
Finished Block Size: *12" x 12" (30 x 30 cm)*

FABRIC REQUIREMENTS

Yardage is based on 43/44" (109/112 cm) wide fabric.

16" x 16" (41 x 41 cm) square of 4 different tan prints

$1^1/4$ yds (1.1 m) of dark tan print

$^1/4$ yd (23 cm) of purple tone-on-tone

$^1/2$ yd (46 cm) of purple print

$^3/8$ yd (34 cm) of purple floral

$^3/8$ yd (34 cm) of blue print

$^1/4$ yd (23 cm) of blue floral

$^3/8$ yd (34 cm) of blue tone-on-tone

18" x 18" (46 x 46 cm) square of green print

$2^7/8$ yds (2.6 m) of backing fabric

You will also need:

51" x 51" (130 x 130 cm) square of batting

CUTTING OUT THE PIECES

Refer to **Rotary Cutting**, *page 64, to cut fabrics. All measurements include a $^1/4$" seam allowance. Background squares and borders are cut larger than needed and will be trimmed after appliquéing. Refer to* **Needleturn Appliqué**, *page 67, to use patterns, page 29.*

From *each* square of tan print:
- Cut 1 background square $14^1/2$" x $14^1/2$".

From dark tan print:
- Cut 4 *crosswise* borders $8^1/2$" x 34".
- Cut 1 strip $4^1/2$" x 23". From this strip, cut 8 rectangles $4^1/2$" x $2^1/2$".
- Cut 2 strips $2^1/2$" x 13".

From purple tone-on-tone:
- Cut 3 strips $2^1/2$" wide. From these strips, cut 47 squares $2^1/2$" x $2^1/2$".

From purple print:
- Cut 24 leaves (**A**).
- Cut 2 squares $2^1/2$" x $2^1/2$".

From purple floral:
- Cut 8 leaves (**A**).
- Cut 4 flower centers (**C**).

From blue print:
- Cut 16 flower petals (**B**).
- Cut 1 strip $2^1/2$" wide. From this strip, cut 10 squares $2^1/2$" x $2^1/2$".

From blue floral:
- Cut 2 strips $2^1/2$" wide. From these strips, cut 30 squares $2^1/2$" x $2^1/2$".
- Cut 1 strip $2^1/2$" x 13".

From blue tone-on-tone:
- Cut 5 binding strips $1^3/4$" wide.

From green print:
- Cut 4 bias stems 1" x 24", piecing as necessary (**D**).

APPLIQUÉING THE BLOCKS AND BORDERS

*Refer to **Assembly Diagram**, page 28, and photo, page 24, for appliqué placement. Refer to **Needleturn Appliqué**, page 67, for appliqué technique.*

1. Fold each background square in half lengthwise, crosswise, and diagonally; finger press folds. Unfold squares and use pressed lines as placement guides. Referring to **Block Diagram**, appliqué leaves, flower petals then flower centers to background squares. Centering appliqués, trim **Blocks** to $12^{1}/_{2}$" x $12^{1}/_{2}$".

Block Diagram (make 4)

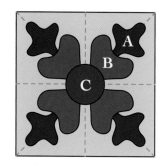

2. Fold each border in half crosswise and lengthwise; finger press folds. Unfold borders and use pressed lines as placement guides, keeping appliqués in a $4^{1}/_{2}$" x $28^{1}/_{2}$" area. Appliqué stems then leaves to borders. Centering appliqués, trim Border **widths** to $6^{1}/_{2}$". Border lengths will be trimmed to fit after measuring completed quilt top center.

Border Diagram (make 4)

ASSEMBLING THE QUILT TOP

*Use a $^{1}/_{4}$" seam allowance and refer to **Piecing and Pressing**, page 65, and **Assembly Diagram**, page 28, to assemble the Quilt Top.*

1. Sew 3 blue print or blue floral squares alternately with 3 purple tone-on-tone squares to make **Short Sashing Row**. Make 6 Short Sashing Rows.

Short Sashing Row (make 6)

2. Sew 8 purple tone-on-tone squares alternately with 7 blue print or blue floral squares to make **Long Sashing Rows 1 and 3**. Sew 7 purple tone-on-tone squares alternately with 8 blue print or blue floral squares to make **Long Sashing Row 2**.

Long Sashing Rows 1 and 3

Long Sashing Row 2

3. Sew 2 Blocks and 3 short Sashing Rows together to make **Row**. Make 2 Rows.

Row (make 2)

4. Sew Long Sashing Row 1, one Row, Long Sashing Row 2, remaining Row, and Long Sashing Row 3 together to complete piecing **Quilt Top Center**.

5. Sew 1 blue floral and 2 dark tan $2^{1}/_{2}$" x 13" strips together to make **Strip Set A**. Cut across Strip Set at $2^{1}/_{2}$" intervals to make 4 **Unit 1's**.

Strip Set A   **Unit 1** (make 4)

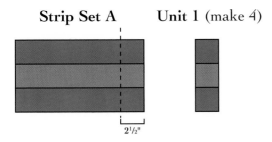

$2^{1}/_{2}$"

6. Sew 1 dark tan $4^{1}/_{2}$" x $2^{1}/_{2}$" rectangle and 1 purple tone-on-tone $2^{1}/_{2}$" x $2^{1}/_{2}$" square together to make **Unit 2**. Make 6 **Unit 2's**. Sew 1 dark tan $4^{1}/_{2}$" x $2^{1}/_{2}$" rectangle and 1 purple print $2^{1}/_{2}$" x $2^{1}/_{2}$" square together to make **Unit 3**. Make 2 **Unit 3's**.

Unit 2 (make 6)   **Unit 3** (make 2)

7. Sew 1 Unit 1 and 2 Unit 2's together to make **Corner Square A**. Make 2 Corner Squares A. Sew 1 Unit 1, 1 Unit 2 and 1 Unit 3 together to make **Corner Square B**. Make 2 Corner Squares B.

Corner Square A (make 2)

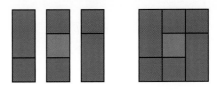

Corner Square B (make 2)

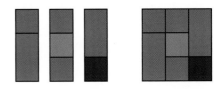

8. Refer to **Adding Borders with Corner Squares**, page 72, to sew borders and corner squares to Quilt Top Center to complete **Quilt Top**.

FINISHING

1. Follow **Quilting**, page 72, to mark, layer and quilt as desired. Our quilt is machine outline quilted around the appliqués and echo quilted in the flower petals. There is meandering quilting in the block backgrounds and borders. There are swirls and wavy lines quilted in the sashings.

2. Follow **Making A Hanging Sleeve**, page 75, to make and then attach a hanging sleeve, if desired.

3. Follow **Binding**, page 76, to sew binding to quilt top using desired method.

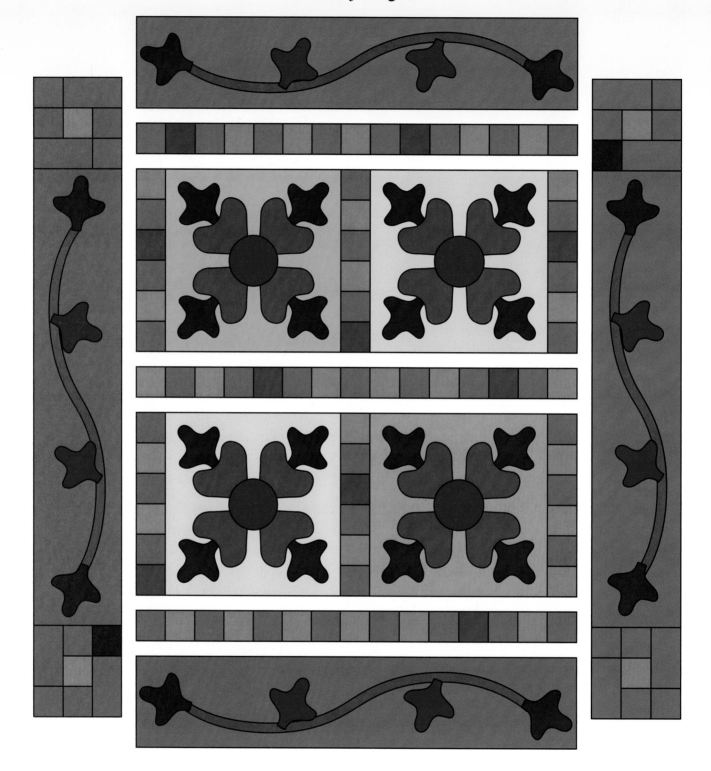

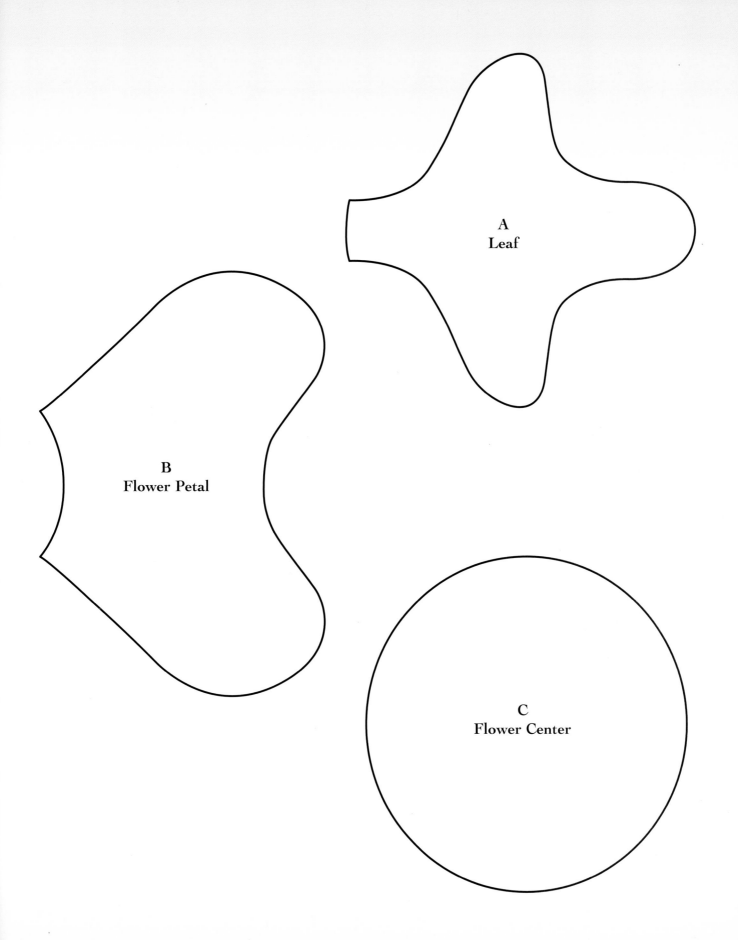

A
Leaf

B
Flower Petal

C
Flower Center

"I had this design and wanted to make a fall quilt, so off to the fabric store I went! The orange flowers were the inspiration for the colors in the quilt. I added deep purple, olive green, and a nice autumn yellow. The border, with its tiny print, was the perfect match!" — Pat

Trumpet BLOOMS

Finished Size: 63" x 63" (160 x 160 cm)
Finished Block Size: 14" x 14" (36 x 36 cm)

FABRIC REQUIREMENTS

Yardage is based on 43/44" (109/112 cm) wide fabric.

 3 yds (2.7 m) of tan floral print
 1 yd (91 cm) of tan plaid
 $^3/_8$ yd (34 cm) of red/orange print
 2 yds (1.8 m) of olive green plaid
 $^3/_4$ yd (69 cm) of olive green print
 $^3/_8$ yd (34 cm) of dark purple print
 $^1/_8$ yd (11 cm) **each** of orange print and
  yellow print
 4 yds (3.7 m) of backing fabric

You will also need:

 Paper-backed fusible web
 71" x 71" (180 x 180 cm) square of batting
 Stabilizer (optional)

CUTTING OUT THE PIECES

Refer to **Rotary Cutting***, page 64, to cut fabrics. All measurements include a $^1/_4$" seam allowance. Borders are cut 4" longer than needed for "insurance" and will be trimmed to correct size after measuring quilt top center. Refer to* **Preparing Fusible Appliqués***, page 68, to use patterns, page 35.*

From tan floral print:
- Cut 2 *lengthwise* top/bottom borders $7^1/_2$" x $52^1/_2$".
- Cut 2 *lengthwise* side borders $7^1/_2$" x $66^1/_2$".
- Cut 4 strips $7^1/_2$" wide. From these strips, cut 18 squares $7^1/_2$" x $7^1/_2$".

From tan plaid:
- Cut 4 strips $7^1/_2$" wide. From these strips, cut 18 squares $7^1/_2$" x $7^1/_2$".

From red/orange print:
- Cut 1 strip 2" wide. From this strip, cut 16 sashing squares 2" x 2".
- Cut 36 flowers (**A**).

From olive green plaid:
- Cut 7 binding strips $1^3/_4$" wide.
- Cut 24 sashing strips 2" x $14^1/_2$".
- Cut 36 stems (**B**).

From olive green print:
- Cut 36 leaves (**F**) and 36 leaves in reverse (**Fr**).

From dark purple print:
- Cut 9 outer circles (**C**).

From orange print:
- Cut 9 middle circles (**D**).

From yellow print:
- Cut 9 inner circles (**E**).

ASSEMBLING THE QUILT TOP

*Use a ¹/4" seam allowance and refer to **Piecing and Pressing**, page 65, and **Assembly Diagram**, page 33, to assemble the Quilt Top. Refer to **Blanket Stitch Appliqué**, page 69, for appliqué technique.*

1. Sew 2 tan floral and 2 tan plaid squares together to make **pieced square**. Make 9 pieced squares.

2. Fold each pieced square in half diagonally; finger press folds. Unfold squares and use seamlines and pressed lines as placement guides. Referring to **Block Diagram**, work in alphabetical order to arrange appliqués on pieced squares; fuse in place. Blanket Stitch around appliqués to complete **Block**. Make 9 Blocks.

Block Diagram (make 9)

3. Sew 4 sashing squares and 3 sashing strips together to make **Sashing Row**. Make 4 Sashing Rows.

Sashing Row (make 4)

4. Sew 4 sashing strips and 3 Blocks together to make **Row**. Make 3 Rows.

Row (make 3)

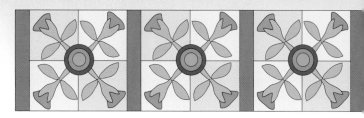

5. Sew 4 Sashing Rows and 3 Rows together to make **Quilt Top Center**.

6. Refer to **Adding Squared Borders**, page 71, to sew top/bottom, then side borders to Quilt Top Center to complete the **Quilt Top**.

FINISHING

1. Follow **Quilting**, page 72, to mark, layer and quilt as desired. Our quilt is machine quilted with outline quilting around the appliqués. There is meadering quilting in the block backgrounds and borders.

2. Follow **Making A Hanging Sleeve**, page 75, to make and then attach a hanging sleeve, if desired.

3. Follow **Binding**, page 76, to sew binding to quilt top using desired method.

Assembly Diagram

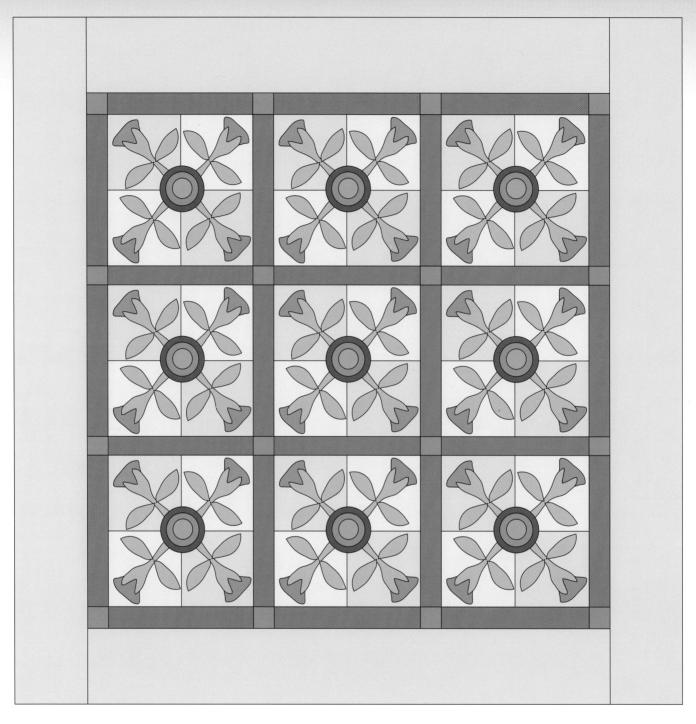

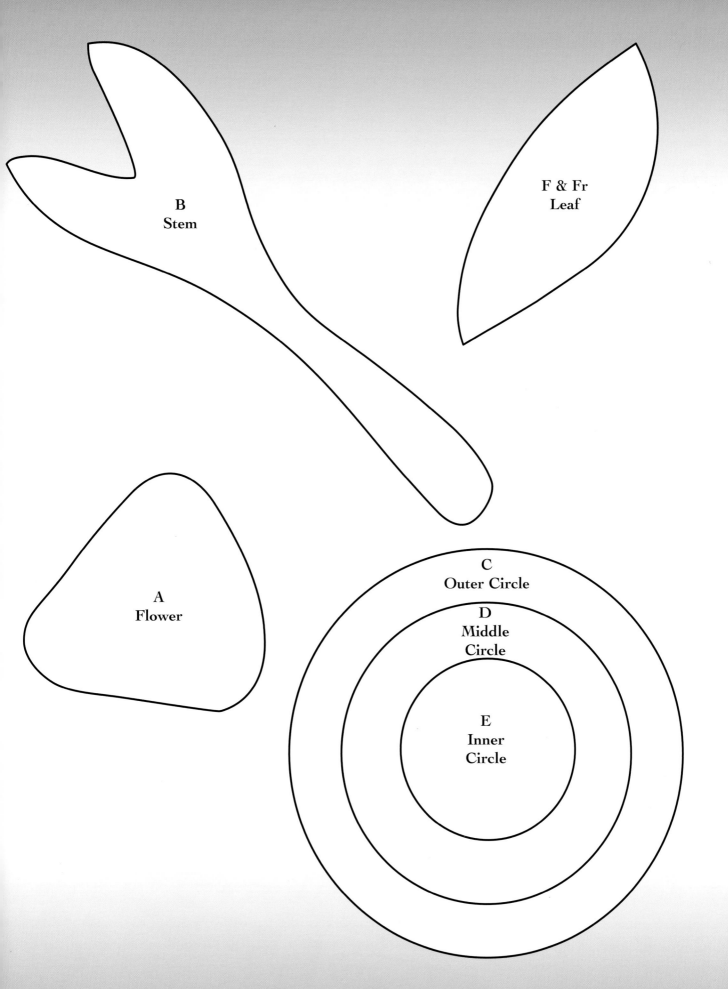

B
Stem

F & Fr
Leaf

A
Flower

C
Outer Circle

D
Middle
Circle

E
Inner
Circle

"Fall means acorns and what better way to show them off than in an autumn quilt. I also love the plaids and found that the wonderful deep greens, combined with golds and browns, made a quilt that speaks of the arrival of fall." — Pat

Acorn CACHE

Finished Size: 52¹/₂" x 52¹/₂" (133 x 133 cm)
Finished Block Size: 12" x 12" (30 x 30 cm)

FABRIC REQUIREMENTS

Yardage is based on 43/44" (109/112 cm) wide fabric.

2¹/₄ yds (2.1 m) of tan/cream stripe
1³/₄ yds (1.6 m) of green/gold plaid
1³/₄ yds (1.6 m) of green tone-on-tone
¹/₄ yd (23 cm) of green/black print
¹/₄ yd (23 cm) of green/black plaid
¹/₂ yd (46 cm) of light gold print
³/₈ yd (34 cm) of dark gold print
1¹/₂ yds (1.4 m) of brown/cream stripe
¹/₈ yd (11 cm) of brown/black plaid
3¹/₂ yds (3.2 m) of backing fabric

You will also need:

Paper-backed fusible web
60" x 60" (152 x 152 cm) square of batting
Stabilizer (optional)

CUTTING OUT THE PIECES

*Refer to **Rotary Cutting**, page 64, to cut fabrics. All measurements include a ¹/₄" seam allowance. Background squares are cut larger than needed and will be trimmed after appliquéing. Borders are cut 4" longer than needed for "insurance" and will be trimmed to correct size after measuring quilt top center. Refer to **Preparing Fusible Appliqués**, page 68, to use patterns, pages 40-41. **Note:** The green/black plaid leaves and the plaid acorn caps are cut on the bias.*

From tan/cream stripe:
- Cut 5 strips 14¹/₂" wide. From these strips, cut 9 background squares 14¹/₂" x 14¹/₂".

From green/gold plaid:
- Cut 2 *lengthwise* side outer borders 4¹/₂" x 56".
- Cut 2 *lengthwise* top/bottom outer borders 4¹/₂" x 48".
- Cut 18 stems (**A**).
- Cut 8 leaves (**B**).

From green tone-on-tone:
- Cut 6 binding strips 1³/₄ wide.
- Cut 2 *lengthwise* side inner borders 2" x 46¹/₂".
- Cut 2 *lengthwise* top/bottom inner borders 2" x 43¹/₂".
- Cut 12 sashing strips 2" x 12¹/₂".
- Cut 12 leaves (**B**).

From green/black print:
- Cut 8 leaves (**B**).

From green/black plaid:
- Cut 8 leaves (**B**).

From light gold print:
- Cut 24 acorns (**C**).
- Cut 7 stars (**E**).

From dark gold print:
- Cut 12 acorns (**C**).
- Cut 6 stars (**E**).
- Cut 4 sashing squares 2" x 2".

From brown/cream stripe:
- Cut 2 *lengthwise* side middle borders 1¹/₄" x 48".
- Cut 2 *lengthwise* top/bottom middle borders 1¹/₄" x 46¹/₂".
- Cut 24 acorn tops (**D**).

From brown/black plaid:
- Cut 12 acorn tops (**D**).

ASSEMBLING THE QUILT TOP

*Use a ¼" seam allowance and refer to **Piecing and Pressing**, page 65, and **Quilt Top Diagram**, page 39, to assemble the Quilt Top. Refer to **Blanket Stitch Appliqué**, page 69, for appliqué technique.*

1. Fold each background square in half lengthwise, crosswise, and diagonally; finger press folds. Unfold squares and use pressed lines as placement guides. Referring to **Block Diagram**, work in alphabetical order to arrange appliqués on background squares; fuse in place.

2. Blanket Stitch around appliqués. Centering appliqués, trim **Blocks** to 12½" x 12½". Make 9 Blocks.

Block Diagram (make 9)

3. Sew 3 Blocks and 2 sashing strips together to make **Row**. Make 3 Rows.

Row (make 3)

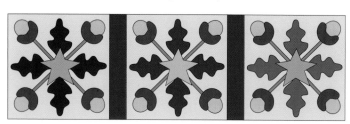

4. Sew 3 sashing strips and 2 sashing squares together to make a **Sashing Row**. Make 2 Sashing Rows.

Sashing Row (make 2)

5. Sew Rows and Sashing Rows together to complete **Quilt Top Center**.

6. Refer to **Adding Squared Borders**, page 71, to sew top/bottom then side inner, middle, and outer borders to Quilt Top Center. Fuse, and then Blanket Stitch 1 Star E on each corner of the **Quilt Top**.

FINISHING

1. Follow **Quilting**, page 72, to mark, layer and quilt as desired. Our quilt is machine outline quilted around the appliqués and sashings. There is meandering quilting in the block backgrounds and a leaf and vine in the borders. There are swirls quilted in the center of each star and detail lines in the acorns.

2. Follow **Making A Hanging Sleeve**, page 75, to make and then attach a hanging sleeve, if desired.

3. Follow **Binding**, page 76, to sew binding to quilt top using desired method.

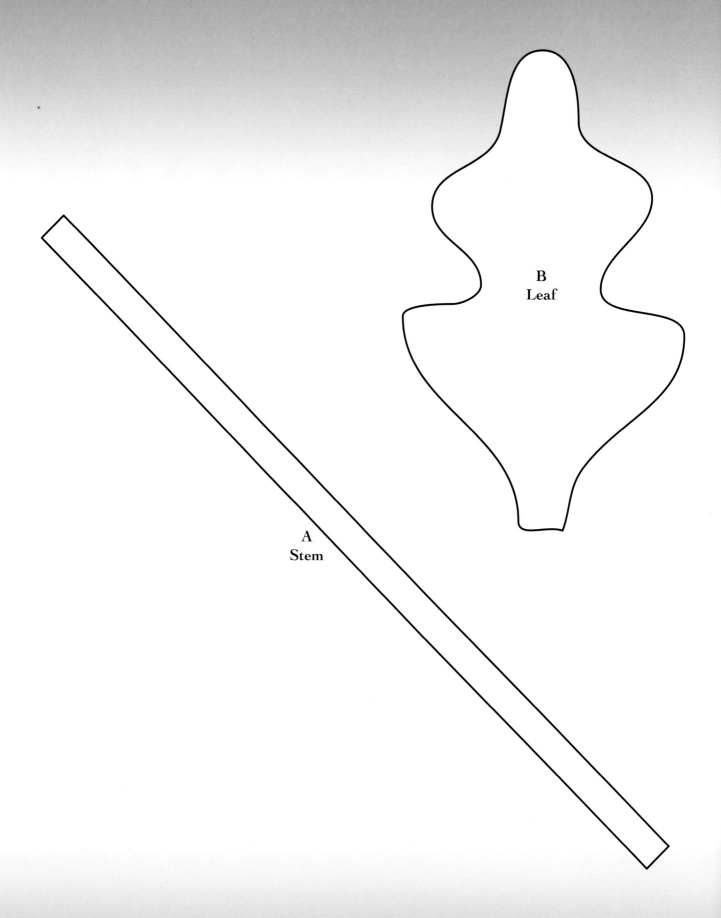

A
Stem

B
Leaf

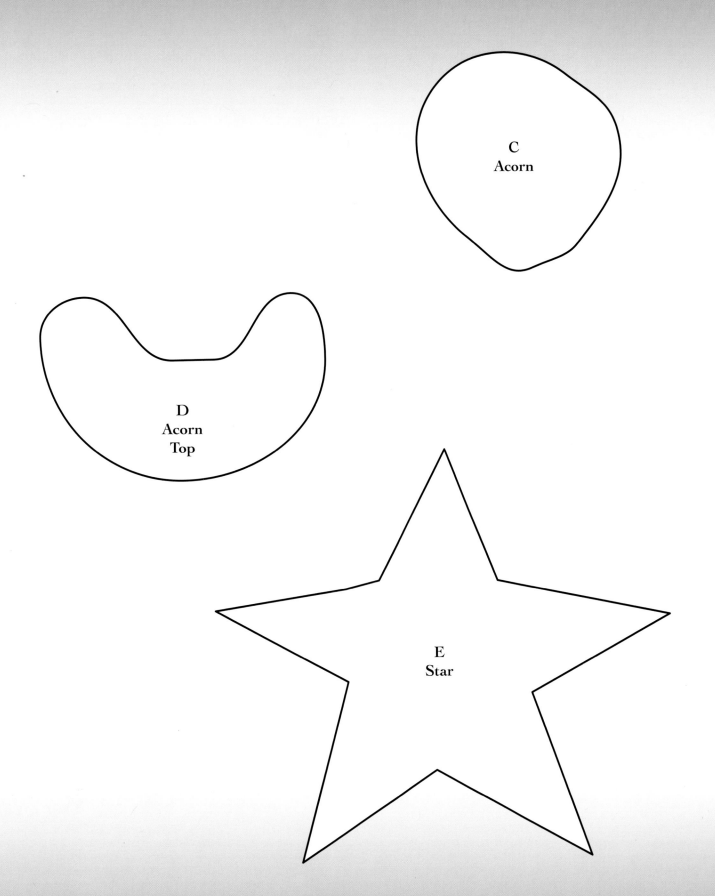

C
Acorn

D
Acorn
Top

E
Star

Vine TRELLIS

Finished Size: 55" x 71" (140 x 180 cm)
Finished Panel Size: 10¹/₂" x 58" (27 x 147 cm)

FABRIC REQUIREMENTS

Yardage is based on 43/44" (109/112 cm) wide fabric.

3⁵/₈ yds (3.3 m) of beige tone-on-tone flannel
⁵/₈ yd (57 cm) of dark green print flannel
¹/₈ yd (11 cm) **each** of 3 assorted green print flannels
2 yds (1.8 m) of green/red floral flannel
1 yd (91 cm) **total** of assorted red print flannels
³/₈ yd (34 cm) of red print flannel
¹/₂ yd (46 cm) of dark red print flannel
4¹/₂ yds (4.1 m) of flannel for backing

You will also need:

Paper-backed fusible web
Water-soluble fabric basting glue
¹/₂" (12 mm) wide bias tape maker (optional)
63" x 79" (160 x 201 cm) rectangle of batting
Stabilizer (optional)

CUTTING OUT THE PIECES

*Refer to **Rotary Cutting**, page 64, to cut fabrics. All measurements include a ¹/₄" seam allowance. Borders are cut 4" longer than needed for "insurance" and will be trimmed to correct size after measuring quilt top center. Background panels are cut larger than needed and will be trimmed after appliquéing. Refer to **Preparing Fusible Appliqués**, page 68, to use patterns, pages 44-45.*

From beige tone-on-tone flannel:
- Cut 3 *lengthwise* appliqué panels 13" x 60¹/₂".
- Cut 2 *lengthwise* sashing strips 2¹/₄" x 58¹/₂"

From dark green print flannel:
- Cut 1 square 20" x 20".

From *each* assorted green print:
- Cut 5 leaves (**D**).

From green/red floral flannel:
- Cut 2 *lengthwise* side outer borders 5¹/₂" x 64¹/₂".
- Cut 2 *lengthwise* top/bottom inner borders 5¹/₂" x 58¹/₂".
- Cut 4 *lengthwise* sashing strips 2¹/₄" x 58¹/₂".

From assorted red print flannels:
- Cut a **total** of 7 binding strips each 1³/₄" x 40, pieced as necessary.
- Cut 15 flowers (**B**).

From red print flannel:
- Cut 2 *crosswise* side inner borders 1¹/₂" x 62¹/₂", piecing as necessary.
- Cut 2 *crosswise* top/bottom inner borders 1¹/₂" x 48¹/₂", piecing as necessary.

From dark red print flannel:
- Cut 15 calyxes (**C**).

"I love large flower shapes and when I designed this quilt, I took that look to the max! This quilt is so quick to make and the flowers make a huge statement. The border of this quilt is a wonderful way to show off a beautiful floral fabric." — Pat

APPLIQUÉING THE PANELS

*Refer to **Assembly Diagram**, page 45, and photo, page 42, for appliqué placement and **Blanket Stitch Appliqué**, page 69, for appliqué technique.*

1. For vines, refer to **Making A Continuous Bias Strip**, page 68, and use dark green print flannel square to make a bias strip 1" wide x 180" long. Cut strip into three 60" lengths (**A**). Press each long edge ¼" to the wrong side or use bias tape maker following the manufacturer's instructions.

2. Fold each appliqué panel in half crosswise and lengthwise; finger press folds. Unfold panels and use pressed lines as placement guides. Arrange stems on panels; use basting glue to temporarily hold stems in place. Working in alphabetical order, and keeping top of appliqués 3" from top edge of panel, arrange remaining appliqués on appliqué panels; fuse appliqués in place. Blanket Stitch around appliqués. Centering appliqués, trim appliqué panels to 11" x 58½". Make 3 Appliqué Panels.

ASSEMBLING THE QUILT TOP

*Use a ¼" seam allowance and refer to **Piecing and Pressing**, page 65, and **Assembly Diagram**, page 45, to assemble the Quilt Top.*

1. Sew 1 beige tone-on-tone and 2 green/red flannel print sashing strips together to make 1 **Sashing Unit**. Make 2 Sashing Units.

2. Sew 3 Appliqué Panels and 2 Sashing Units together to complete **Quilt Top Center**.

3. Refer to **Adding Squared Borders**, page 71, to sew side then top/bottom inner and outer borders to Quilt Top Center to complete the **Quilt Top**.

FINISHING

1. Follow **Quilting**, page 72, to mark, layer and quilt as desired. Our quilt is machine outline quilted around the appliqués and Sashing Units. There is meandering quilting in the Appliqué Panels and outer borders.

2. Follow **Making A Hanging Sleeve**, page 75, to make and then attach a hanging sleeve, if desired.

3. Follow **Binding**, page 76, to sew binding to quilt top using desired method.

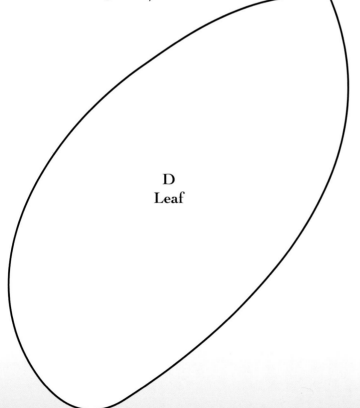

D
Leaf

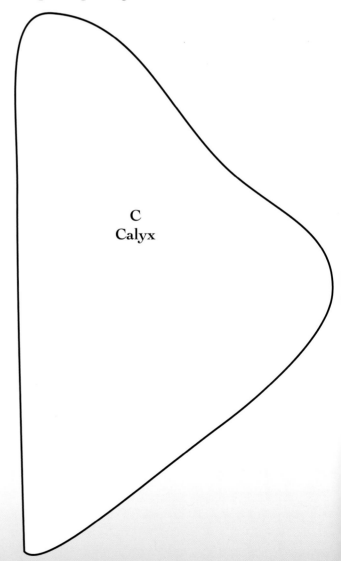

C
Calyx

Assembly Diagram

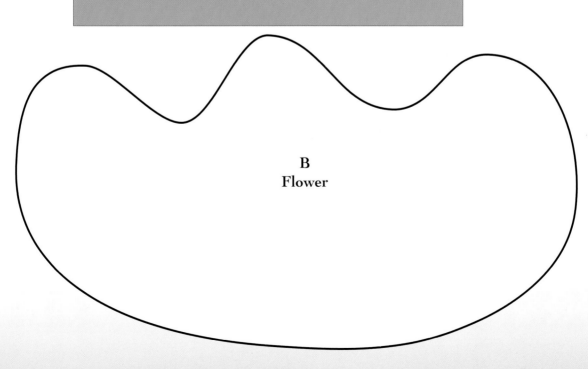

B
Flower

Budding BEAUTY

Finished Size: $50\frac{1}{2}$" x $50\frac{1}{2}$" (128 x 128 cm)
Finished Block Size: 16" x 16" (41 x 41 cm)

FABRIC REQUIREMENTS

Yardage is based on 43/44" (109/112 cm) wide fabric.

$1\frac{1}{8}$ yds (1.0 m) of white/red print
$1\frac{1}{2}$ yds (1.3 m) of green print
$1\frac{7}{8}$ yds (1.7 m) of red/black print
$\frac{1}{8}$ yd (11 cm) of gold print
$\frac{1}{2}$ yd (46 cm) of red/tan stripe
$3\frac{1}{4}$ yds (3.0 m) of backing fabric

You will also need:

Paper-backed fusible web
58" x 58" (147 x 147 cm) square of batting
Stabilizer (optional)

CUTTING OUT THE PIECES

*Refer to **Rotary Cutting**, page 64, to cut fabrics. All measurements include a $\frac{1}{4}$" seam allowance. Background squares and borders are cut larger than needed and will be trimmed after appliquéing. Refer to **Preparing Fusible Appliqués**, page 68, to use patterns, page 51.*

From white/red print:
- Cut 2 strips $18\frac{1}{2}$" wide. From these strips, cut 4 background squares $18\frac{1}{2}$" x $18\frac{1}{2}$".

From green print:
- Cut 9 squares 2" x 2".
- Cut 24 leaves (**A**).
- Cut 16 stems (**C**).
- Cut 6 binding strips $1\frac{3}{4}$" wide.

From red/black print:
- Cut 2 *lengthwise* top/bottom borders 9" x 41".
- Cut 2 *lengthwise* side borders 9" x 54".
- Cut 16 buds (**B**).
- Cut 4 circles (**D**).

From gold print:
- Cut 8 stars (**E**).

From red/tan stripe:
- Cut 6 strips 2" wide. From these strips, cut 12 sashing strips 2" x $16\frac{1}{2}$".
- Cut 4 circles (**D**).

"I love antique quilts and was inspired by old quilts with simple blocks. The wonderful red toile and other fabrics in this quilt are reproductions of old fabrics. I added stars, repeated the block, then made a wide border with stars and ferns." — Pat

ASSEMBLING THE QUILT TOP

Use a ¹/₄" seam allowance and refer to **Piecing and Pressing**, *page 65, and* **Assembly Diagram**, *page 49, to assemble the Quilt Top. Refer to* **Blanket Stitch Appliqué**, *page 69, for appliqué technique.*

1. Fold each background square in half lengthwise, crosswise, and diagonally; finger press folds. Unfold squares and use pressed lines as placement guides. Referring to **Block Diagram**, work in alphabetical order to arrange appliqués on background squares; fuse in place. Blanket Stitch around appliqués. Centering appliqués, trim **Blocks** to 16¹/₂" x 16¹/₂".

Block Diagram (make 4)

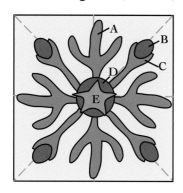

2. Fold each border in half crosswise and lengthwise; finger press folds. Unfold borders and use pressed lines as placement guides. Referring to **Border Diagram**, work in alphabetical order to arrange appliqués on borders; fuse in place. Blanket Stitch around appliqués. Centering appliqués, trim Border **width** to 7". Border lengths will be trimmed to fit after measuring completed quilt top center.

Border Diagram (make 4)

3. Sew 3 sashing strips and 2 Blocks together to make **Row**. Make 2 Rows.

Row (make 2)

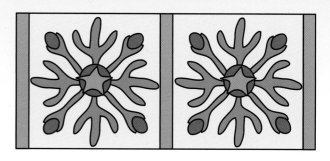

4. Sew 2 sashing strips and 3 green squares together to make a **Sashing Row**. Make 3 Sashing Rows.

Sashing Row (make 3)

5. Sew Rows and Sashing Rows together to complete **Quilt Top Center**.
6. Refer to **Adding Squared Borders**, page 71, to sew top/bottom then side borders to Quilt Top Center to complete the **Quilt Top**.

FINISHING

1. Follow **Quilting**, page 72, to mark, layer and quilt as desired. Our quilt is machine outline quilted around the appliqués and sashings. There is meandering in the block backgrounds and borders.
2. Follow **Making A Hanging Sleeve**, page 75, to make and then attach a hanging sleeve, if desired.
3. Follow **Binding**, page 76, to sew binding to quilt top using desired method.

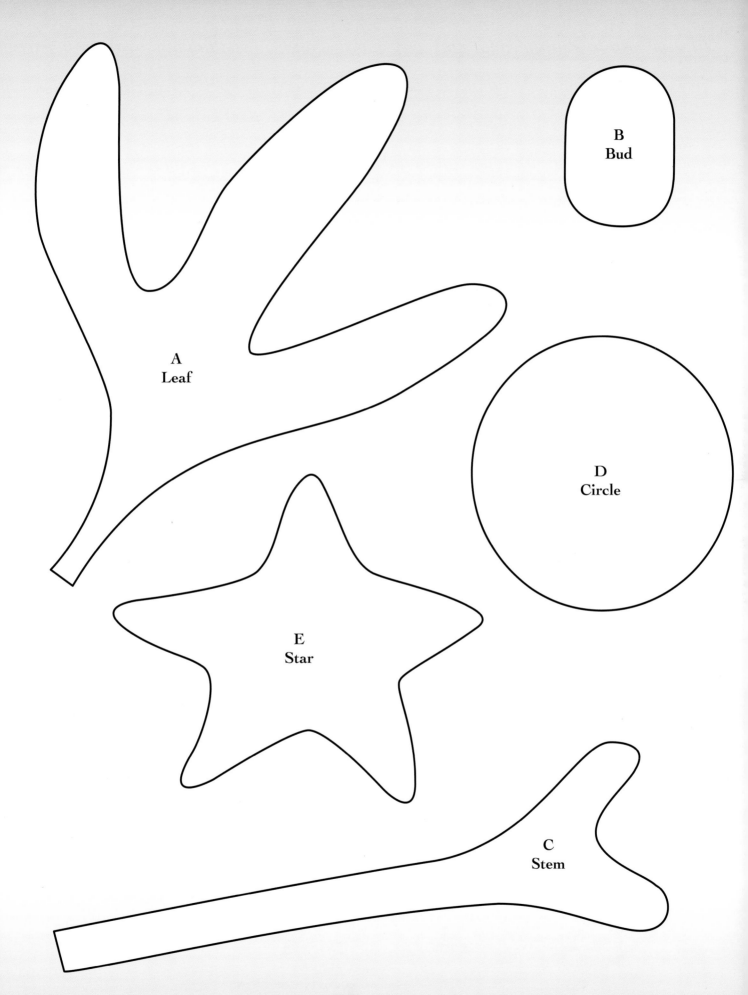

B
Bud

A
Leaf

D
Circle

E
Star

C
Stem

"I was born in Pennsylvania and spent many summers visiting my great-grandparents in Lancaster. I wanted to make a quilt that reminded me of the area. Many quilts from Pennsylvania have a red/green color combination, so I selected that for my very folky flower branches. I think this quilt would be really dramatic done on a black background, or even in all pastels." — Pat

August BLOOMS

Finished Size: 54" x 54" (137 x 137 cm)
Finished Block Size: 20" x 20" (51 x 51 cm)

FABRIC REQUIREMENTS

Yardage is based on 43/44" (109/112 cm) wide fabric.
  2$\frac{1}{4}$ yds (2.1 m) **each** of light gold prints
    No. 1 and No. 2
  $\frac{1}{2}$ yd (46 cm) of green print
  $\frac{3}{4}$ yd (69 cm) of green stripe
  1 yd (91 cm) of red print
  $\frac{3}{8}$ yd (34 cm) **each** of medium gold print and
    navy print
  3$\frac{1}{2}$ yds (3.2 m) of backing fabric
You will also need:
  Paper-backed fusible web
  Water-soluble fabric basting glue
  62" x 62" (157 x 157 cm) square of batting
  Stabilizer (optional)

CUTTING OUT THE PIECES

*Refer to **Rotary Cutting**, page 64, to cut fabrics. All measurements include a $\frac{1}{4}$" seam allowance. Background squares are cut larger than needed and will be trimmed after appliquéing. Refer to **Preparing Fusible Appliqués**, page 68, to use patterns, pages 57-59.*

From light gold print No. 1:
- Cut 2 background squares 22$\frac{1}{2}$" x 22$\frac{1}{2}$".
- Cut 2 top/bottom borders 5$\frac{1}{2}$" x 22".
- Cut 2 side border strips 5$\frac{1}{2}$" x 27".
- Cut 2 strips 2" wide. From these strips, cut 12 rectangles 2" x 4$\frac{1}{2}$".

From light gold print No. 2:
- Cut 2 background squares 22$\frac{1}{2}$" x 22$\frac{1}{2}$".
- Cut 2 top/bottom border strips 5$\frac{1}{2}$" x 22".
- Cut 2 side border strips 5$\frac{1}{2}$" x 27".
- Cut 1 strip 2" wide. From this strip, cut 8 rectangles 2" x 4$\frac{1}{2}$" and 2 squares 2" x 2".

From green print:
- Cut 4 stems 1$\frac{1}{4}$" x 24".
- Cut 4 stems 1$\frac{1}{4}$" x 18".
- Cut 24 leaves (**C**).

From green stripe:
- Cut 4 leaves (**D**) and 4 leaves reversed (**Dr**).
- Cut 4 leaves (**E**) and 4 leaves reversed (**Er**).

From red print:
- Cut 3 strips 2" wide. From these strips, cut 20 rectangles 2" x 4$\frac{1}{2}$" and 2 squares 2" x 2".
- Cut 6 binding strips 1$\frac{3}{4}$" wide.
- Cut 4 flowers (**F**).
- Cut 12 flowers (**I**).

From medium gold print:
- Cut 4 circles (**G**).
- Cut 12 ovals (**J**).

From navy print:
- Cut 4 medium stars (**H**).
- Cut 12 small stars (**K**).
- Cut 16 large stars (**L**).

ASSEMBLING THE QUILT TOP

*Use a ¼" seam allowance and refer to **Piecing and Pressing**, page 65, and **Assembly Diagram**, page 55, to assemble the Quilt Top. Refer to **Blanket Stitch Appliqué**, page 69, for appliqué technique.*

1. For stems, press each long edge of stems (**A** and **B**) ¼" to the wrong side.
2. Fold each background square in half lengthwise, crosswise, and diagonally; finger press folds. Unfold squares. Using pressed lines as placement guides and referring to **Block Diagram**, work in alphabetical order to position appliqués on squares; use basting glue to temporarily hold stems in place. Blanket Stitch around appliqués. Centering appliqués, trim **Blocks** to 20½" x 20½". Make 4 Blocks.

Block Diagram (make 4)

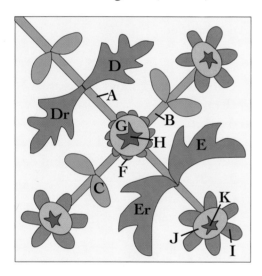

3. Sew 4 Blocks together to make **Quilt Top Center**.

4. Alternating colors, sew 5 red rectangles, 3 light gold No. 1 rectangles, and 2 light gold No. 2 rectangles together to make **Inner Side Border**. Make 2 Inner Side Borders.
5. Alternating colors, sew 5 red rectangles, 3 light gold No. 1 rectangles, 2 light gold No. 2 rectangles, 1 red square, and 1 light gold No. 2 square together to make **Inner Top Border**. Repeat to make **Inner Bottom Border**.
6. Sew Inner Side Borders, then Inner Top/Bottom Borders to Quilt Top Center.
7. Sew 1 light gold No. 1 side border strip and 1 light gold No. 2 side border strip together to make **Outer Side Border**. Make 2 Outer Side Borders.
8. Sew 1 light gold No. 1 top/bottom border strip and 1 light gold No. 2 top/bottom border strip together to make **Outer Top Border**. Repeat to make **Outer Bottom Border**.
9. Position 4 stars (**L**) on each Outer Border; fuse in place. Blanket Stitch around appliqués.
10. Sew Outer Top/Bottom Borders, then Outer Side Borders to pieced center to complete the **Quilt Top**.

FINISHING

1. Follow **Quilting**, page 72, to mark, layer and quilt as desired. Our quilt is machine outline quilted around the appliqués. The leaves are accented with vein lines and the stems with wavy lines. There is meandering in the block backgrounds and borders.
2. Follow **Making A Hanging Sleeve**, page 75, to make and then attach a hanging sleeve, if desired.
3. Follow **Binding**, page 76, to sew binding to quilt top using desired method.

Assembly Diagram

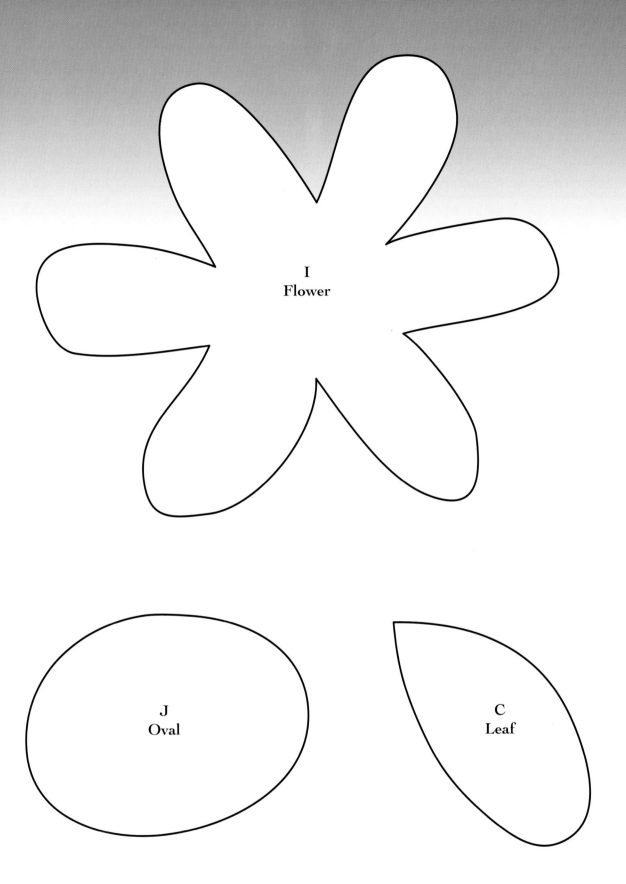

I
Flower

J
Oval

C
Leaf

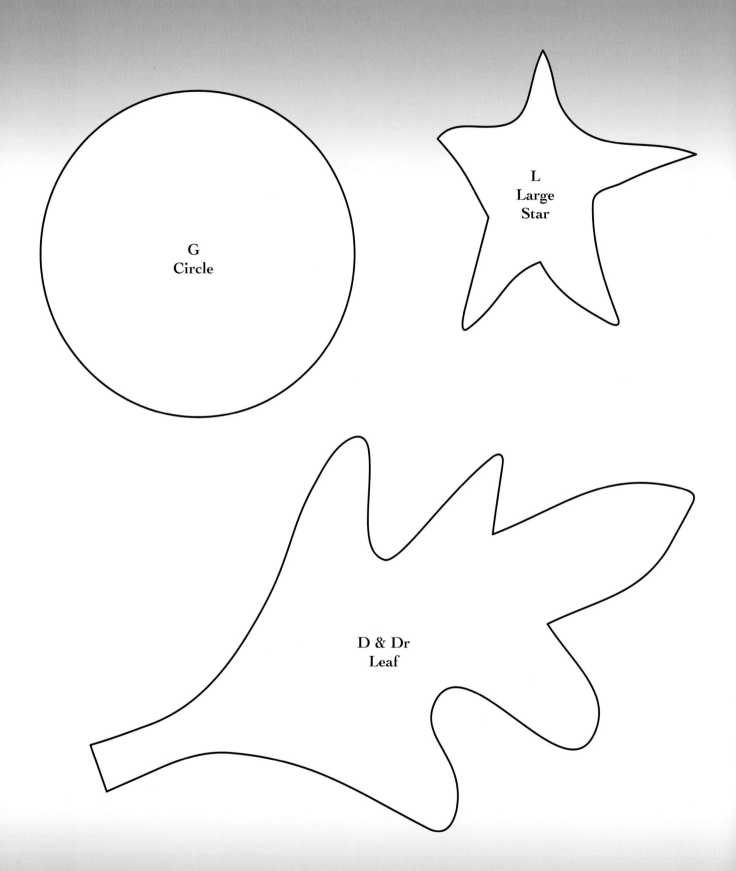

G
Circle

L
Large
Star

D & Dr
Leaf

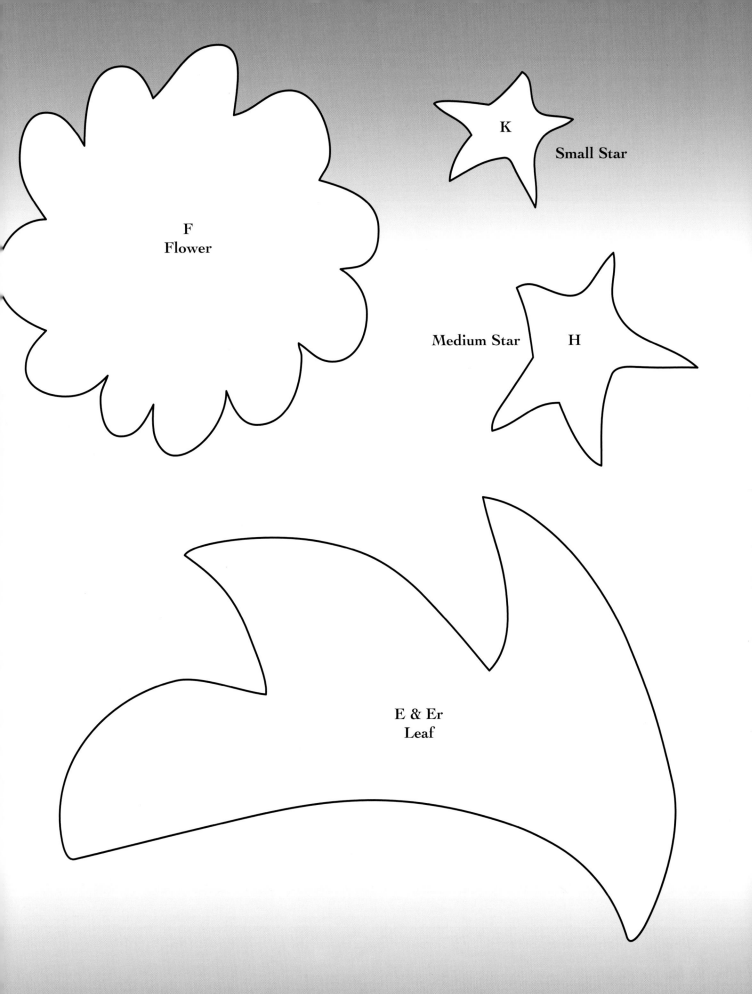

F
Flower

K
Small Star

Medium Star   H

E & Er
Leaf

Dancing SNOWFLAKES

Finished Size: 46" x 55" (117 x 140 cm)
Finished Block Size: 9" x 9" (23 x 23 cm)

FABRIC REQUIREMENTS

Yardage is based on 43/44" (109/112 cm) wide fabric.
   1⁷/₈ yds (1.7 m) **total** of assorted red prints
   1¹/₈ yds (1.1 m) **total** of assorted gold prints
   1¹/₈ yds (1.0 m) **total** of assorted beige prints
   ³/₈ yd (34 cm) of binding fabric
   3¹/₂ yds (3.2 m) of backing fabric
You will also need:
   Paper-backed fusible web
   54" x 63" (137 x 160 cm) rectangle of batting
   Stabilizer

CUTTING OUT THE PIECES

*Refer to **Rotary Cutting**, page 64, to cut fabrics. All measurements include a ¹/₄" seam allowance. Refer to **Preparing Fusible Appliqués**, page 68, to use snowflake pattern, page 62.*

From assorted red prints:
   • Cut 20 pairs of like print strips 3¹/₂" x 9¹/₂".
   • Cut 18 squares 5³/₈" x 5³/₈".
   • Cut 4 corner squares 5" x 5" from like print.
From assorted gold prints:
   • Cut 20 strips 3¹/₂" x 9¹/₂".
   • Cut 18 squares 5³/₈" x 5³/₈".
From assorted beige prints:
   • Cut 30 snowflakes.
From binding fabric:
   • Cut 6 binding strips 1³/₄" wide.

"Every fall, fabric companies come out with really wonderful Christmas collections, and I love buying them! I thought this collection from RJR was really nice and the old-fashioned rail fence block was a perfect way to show it off. After the background was done, it seemed to just 'need' some snowflakes, so I added a flurry of them." — Pat

ASSEMBLING THE QUILT TOP

*Use a ¹/₄" seam allowance and refer to **Piecing and Pressing**, page 65, and **Quilt Top Diagram**, page 63, to assemble the Quilt Top. Refer to **Blanket Stitch Appliqué**, page 69, for appliqué technique.*

1. Sew 2 like red print strips and 1 gold print strip together to make **Block**. Make 20 Blocks.

Block (make 20)

2. Alternating orientation of Blocks, sew 4 Blocks together to make a **Row**. Make 5 Rows. Sew Rows together to make **Quilt Top Center**.

3. Follow **Making Triangle-Squares**, page 66, to make 36 **Triangle-Squares** using assorted red and gold 5³/₈" squares.

Triangle-Square (make 36)

4. Sew 10 Triangle-Squares together to make **Side Border**. Make 2 Side Borders.

5. Sew 8 Triangle-Squares and 2 red print corner squares together to make **Top Border**. Repeat to make **Bottom Border**.

6. Sew Side Borders, then Top/Bottom borders to Quilt Top Center.

7. Position snowflakes on intersections of blocks and on block/border intersections; fuse in place. Follow **Blanket Stitch Appliqué**, page 69, to stitch around snowflakes to complete the **Quilt Top**.

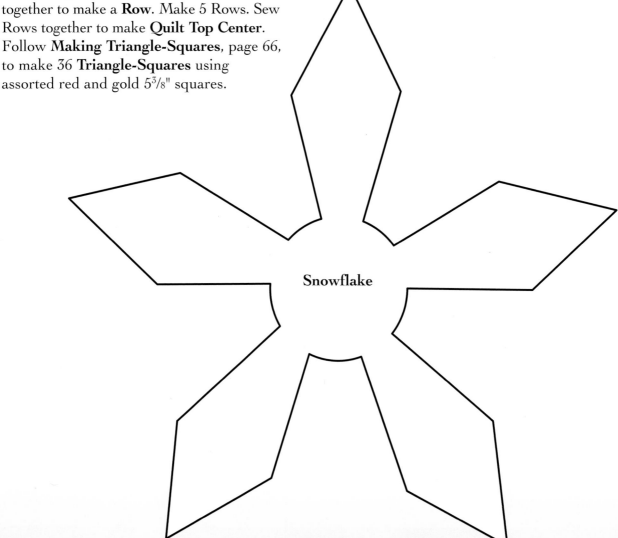

Snowflake

FINISHING

1. Follow **Quilting**, page 72, to mark, layer and quilt as desired. Our quilt is machine quilted with an all over meandering pattern.

2. Follow **Making A Hanging Sleeve**, page 75, to make and then attach a hanging sleeve, if desired.

3. Follow **Binding**, page 76, to sew binding to quilt top using desired method.

Quilt Top Diagram

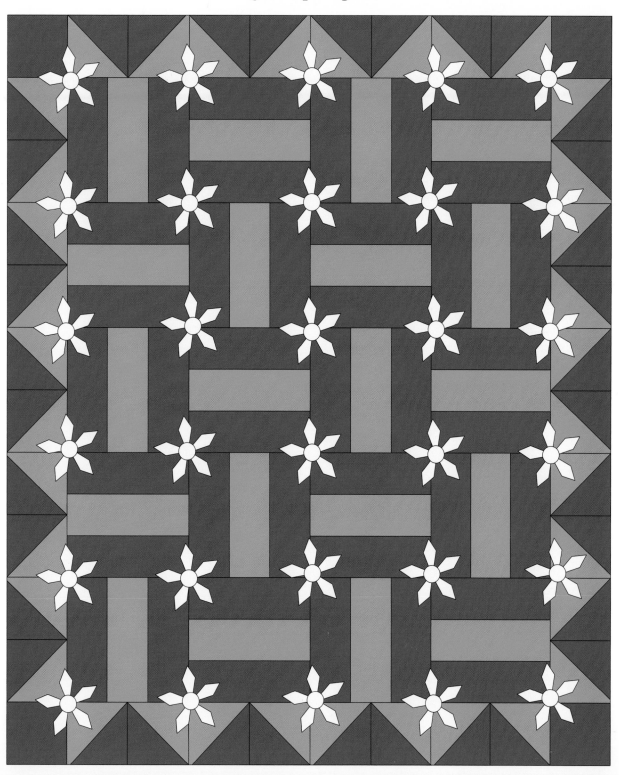

General INSTRUCTIONS

To make your quilting easier and more enjoyable, we encourage you to carefully read all of the general instructions, study the color photographs, and familiarize yourself with the individual project instructions before beginning a project.

FABRICS

SELECTING FABRICS

- Choose good quality medium-weight 100% cotton fabrics. Avoid fabrics that are loosely woven or stretchy. Cotton fabrics are easy to sew, and seam allowances will stay flat when pressed.
- Yardage requirements listed for each project are based on 43/44" wide fabric. After washing and trimming off the selvages, actual usable width is usually 40". The recommended yardages include this shrinkage, but it never hurts to buy a little extra.

PREPARING FABRICS

We recommend that all fabrics be washed, dried, and pressed before cutting. If fabrics are not pre-washed, washing the finished quilt will cause shrinkage and give it a more "antiqued" look and feel. Bright and dark colors, which may run, should always be washed before cutting. After washing and drying fabric, fold lengthwise with wrong sides together and matching selvages.

ROTARY CUTTING

Rotary cutting has brought speed and accuracy to quiltmaking by allowing quilters to easily cut strips of fabric and then cut those strips into smaller pieces.

- Place fabric on work surface with fold closest to you.

- Cut all strips from the selvage-to-selvage width of the fabric unless otherwise indicated in project instructions.

- Square left edge of fabric using rotary cutter and rulers (**Figs. 1 - 2**).

Fig. 1

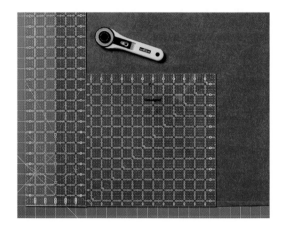

Fig. 2

- To cut each strip required for a project, place ruler over cut edge of fabric, aligning desired marking on ruler with cut edge; make cut (**Fig. 3**).

Fig. 3

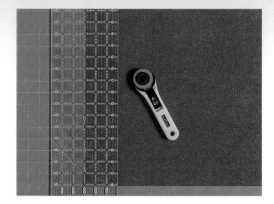

- When cutting several strips from a single piece of fabric, it is important to make sure that cuts remain at a perfect right angle to the fold; square fabric as needed.

PIECING AND PRESSING

PIECING

- Set sewing machine stitch length for approximately 11 stitches per inch.

- Use neutral-colored cotton sewing thread (not quilting thread) in needle and in bobbin.

- An accurate $\frac{1}{4}$" seam allowance is *essential*. Presser feet that are $\frac{1}{4}$" wide are available for most sewing machines. The measurement from the needle to the outer edge of your presser foot should be $\frac{1}{4}$". If this is the case with your machine, your presser foot is your best guide. If not, measure $\frac{1}{4}$" from the needle (a ruler or a piece of graph paper with a $\frac{1}{4}$" grid makes a handy measuring tool) and mark the throat plate with a piece of masking tape (**Fig. 4**).

Fig. 4

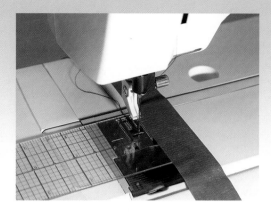

- When piecing, always place pieces right sides together and match raw edges; pin if necessary (**Fig. 5**). (If using pins, remove the pins just before they reach the sewing machine needle.)

Fig. 5

- Chain piecing saves time and will usually result in more accurate piecing.

- Trim away points of seam allowances that extend beyond edges of sewn pieces.

Sewing Across Seam Intersections

When sewing across intersection of two seams, place pieces right sides together and match seams exactly, making sure seam allowances are pressed in opposite directions (**Fig. 6**).

Fig. 6

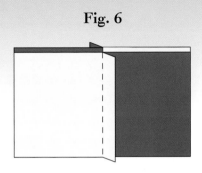

Sewing Sharp Points

To ensure sharp points when joining triangular or diagonal pieces, stitch across the center of the "X" (shown in pink) formed on wrong side by previous seams (**Fig. 7**).

Fig. 7

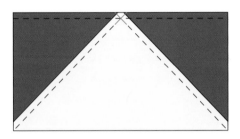

Making Triangle-Squares

1. To make triangle-squares, place 2 squares, right sides together. On wrong side of lighter square, draw a diagonal line across the square. Stitch seam ¹/₄" on each side of drawn line (**Fig. 8**).

Fig. 8

2. Cut on drawn line to make 2 triangle-squares (**Fig. 9**). Open and press seam allowances toward the darker fabric.

Fig. 9

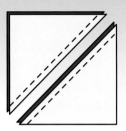

Trimming Seam Allowances

When piecing, some seam allowances may extend beyond the edges of the sewn pieces. Trim away "dog ears" that extend beyond the edges of the sewn pieces (**Fig. 10**).

Fig. 10

PRESSING

- Use steam iron set on "Cotton" for all pressing.

- Pressing differs from ironing in that you do not slide the iron back and forth across the fabric. To press, lift the iron from one section to the next to avoid stretching or distorting the fabric.

- Press after sewing each seam.

- Seam allowances are almost always pressed to one side, usually toward darker fabric. However, to reduce bulk it may occasionally be necessary to press seam allowances toward the lighter fabric or even to press them open.

- To prevent dark fabric seam allowance from showing through light fabric, trim darker seam allowance slightly narrower than lighter seam allowance.

- To press long seams, such as those in long strip sets, without curving or other distortion, lay strips across width of the ironing board.

APPLIQUÉ

NEEDLETURN APPLIQUÉ

Using a needle to turn under seam allowance while blindstitching appliqué to background fabric is called "needleturn appliqué." Patterns for appliqué templates do not include seam allowances.

1. To make a template from a pattern, use a permanent fine-point marker or pen to carefully trace the pattern onto template plastic, making sure to label the template and to transfer any alignment or grain line markings. Check your template against the original pattern for accuracy.
2. Place templates on right side of appliqué fabric. Lightly draw around templates with a pencil, leaving at least $1/2$" between shapes. Cut out shapes approximately $3/16$" outside drawn line. Clip inside curves and points up to, but not through drawn line.
3. Arrange prepared shapes on background fabric and pin or baste in place. Thread a sharps needle with a single strand of cotton sewing thread that matches appliqué; knot one end.
4. Begin blindstitching on as straight an edge as possible, turning a small section of the seam allowance to wrong side with needle, concealing drawn line (**Fig. 11**).

Fig. 11

5. To stitch outward points, stitch to $1/2$" from point (**Fig. 12**). Turn seam allowance under at point (**Fig. 13**); then turn remainder of seam allowance between stitching and point. Stitch to point, taking 2 or 3 stitches at top of point to secure. Turn under small amount of seam allowance past point and resume stitching.

Fig. 12   **Fig. 13**

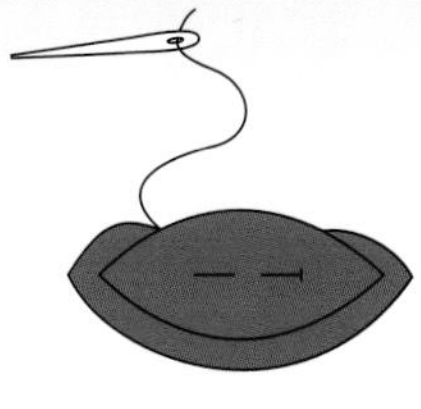

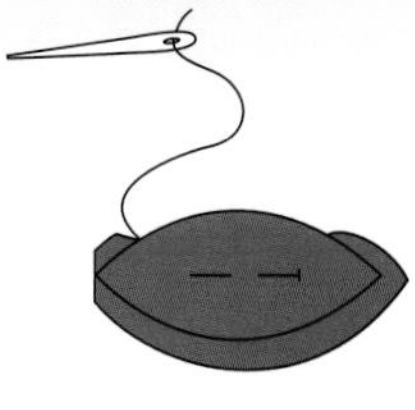

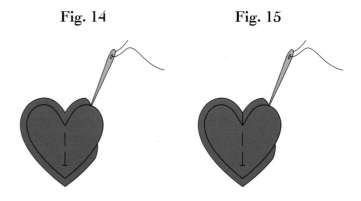

6. To stitch inward point, stitch to $1/2$" from point (**Fig. 14**). Clip to but not through seam allowance at point (**Fig. 15**). Turn seam allowance under between stitching and point. Stitch to point, taking 2 or 3 stitches at point to secure. Turn under small amount of seam allowance past point and resume stitching.

Fig. 14   **Fig. 15**

7. Do not turn under or stitch seam allowances that will be covered by other appliqué pieces.
8. To appliqué pressed bias strips, baste strips in place and blindstitch along edges.
9. To reduce bulk, background fabric behind appliqués may be cut away. After stitching appliqués in place, turn block over and use sharp scissors or specially designed appliqué scissors to trim away background fabric approximately $3/16$" from stitching line. Take care not to cut appliqué fabric or stitches.

PREPARING FUSIBLE APPLIQUÉS

Patterns for fused appliqués are printed in reverse to enable you to use our speedy method of preparing appliqués. If the instructions call for a pattern to be cut in reverse it is because the shape will be used facing both directions; use a black fine-point marker to trace the pattern onto plain white paper, flip paper over and follow Steps 1-4 (below) to trace pattern onto web from the "wrong" side of the paper.

1. Place paper-backed fusible web, web side down, over appliqué pattern. Use a pencil to trace pattern onto paper side of web as many times as indicated in project instructions for a single fabric. (***Note:*** Some pieces may be given as measurements, such as a 2" x 4" rectangle instead of drawn patterns. Draw shape onto paper side of web). Repeat for additional patterns and fabrics.

2. To reduce stiffness when appliquéing, cut away the center of the fusible web ¹/₄" inside the traced or drawn line. Do not cut on the line (**Fig. 16**). It may not be necessary to cut away the center of small or narrow pieces.

Fig. 16

3. Follow manufacturer's instructions to fuse traced patterns to wrong side of fabrics. Do not remove paper backing.

4. Cut out appliqué pieces along traced or drawn lines (**Fig. 17**). Remove paper backing from pieces (**Fig. 18**).

Fig. 17

Fig. 18

MAKING A CONTINUOUS BIAS STRIP

Bias strips for appliqué can simply be cut and pieced to desired length. However, when a long length of bias is needed, the "continuous" method is quick and accurate.

1. Cut square from fabric the size indicated in project instructions. Cut square in half diagonally to make 2 triangles.

2. With right sides together and using a ¼" seam allowance, sew triangles together (**Fig. 19**); press seam allowances open.

Fig. 19

3. On wrong side of fabric, draw lines the width specified in project instructions, (**Fig. 20**). Cut off any remaining fabric less than this width.

Fig. 20

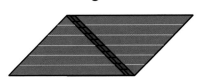

4. With right sides inside, bring short edges together to form tube; match raw edges so that first drawn line of top section meets second drawn line of bottom section (**Fig. 21**).

Fig. 21

5. Carefully pin edges together by inserting pins through drawn lines at point where drawn lines intersect, making sure pins go through intersections on both sides. Using a ¼" seam allowance, sew edges together; press seam allowances open.

6. To cut continuous strip, begin cutting along first drawn line (**Fig. 22**). Continue cutting along drawn line around tube.

Fig. 22

BLANKET STITCH APPLIQUÉ

Some sewing machines feature a Blanket Stitch similar to the one used in this book. Refer to your owner's manual for machine set-up. If your machine does not have this stitch, try any of the decorative stitches your machine has until you are satisfied with the look.

1. Thread sewing machine and bobbin with 100% cotton thread in desired weight.

2. Attach an open-toe presser foot. Select far right needle position and needle down (if your machine has these features).

3. If desired, pin a commercial stabilizer to wrong side of background fabric or spray wrong side of background fabric with starch to stabilize.

4. Bring bobbin thread to the top of the fabric by lowering then raising the needle, bringing up the bobbin thread loop. Pull the loop all the way to the surface.

5. Begin by stitching 5 or 6 stitches in place (drop feed dogs or set stitch length at 0) or, use your machine's lock stitch feature, if equipped, to anchor thread. Return settings to selected Blanket Stitch.

6. Most of the Blanket Stitch should be done on the appliqué with the right edges of the stitch falling at the very outside edge of the appliqué. Stitch over all exposed raw edges of appliqué pieces. **(Note: Dots on Figs 23-27 indicate where to leave needle in fabric when pivoting.)**

7. Always stopping with needle down in background fabric, refer to **Fig. 23** to stitch outside points like tips of leaves. Stop one stitch short of point. Raise presser foot. Pivot project slightly, lower presser foot, and make one angled **Stitch 1**. Take next stitch, stop at point, and pivot so **Stitch 2** will be perpendicular to point. Pivot slightly to make **Stitch 3**. Continue stitching.

Fig. 23

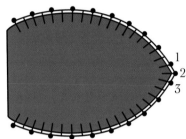

8. For outside corners (**Fig. 24**), stitch to corner, stopping with needle in background fabric. Raise presser foot. Pivot project, lower presser foot, and take an angled stitch. Raise presser foot. Pivot project, lower presser foot and stitch adjacent side.

Fig. 24

9. For inside corners (**Fig. 25**), stitch to the corner, taking the last bite at corner and stopping with the needle down in background fabric. Raise presser foot. Pivot project, lower presser foot, and take an angled stitch. Raise presser foot. Pivot project, lower presser foot and stitch adjacent side.

Fig. 25

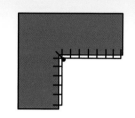

10. When stitching outside curves (**Fig. 26**), stop with needle down in background fabric. Raise presser foot and pivot project as needed. Lower presser foot and continue stitching, pivoting as often as necessary to follow curve. Small circles may require pivoting between each stitch.

Fig. 26

11. When stitching inside curves (**Fig. 27**), stop with needle down in background fabric. Raise presser foot and pivot project as needed. Lower presser foot and continue stitching, pivoting as often as necessary to follow curve.

Fig. 27

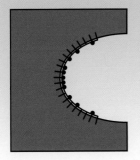

12. When stopping stitching, use a lock stitch to sew 5 or 6 stitches in place or use a needle to pull threads to wrong side of background fabric (**Fig. 28**); knot, then trim ends.

Fig. 28

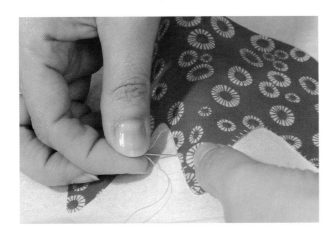

13. Carefully tear away stabilizer, if used.

BORDERS

*Borders cut along the lengthwise grain will lie flatter than borders cut along the crosswise grain. Most of the quilts in this book have the top/bottom borders added first. **Note:** If your project instructions call for the **side** borders to be added first, reverse Steps 2 and 3 by measuring the **length** through the middle of the quilt top center; trim side borders and sew side borders to Quilt Top Center. Measure **width** through middle of Quilt Top Center, including side borders; trim top/bottom borders and sew to Quilt Top Center.*

ADDING SQUARED BORDERS

1. Mark the center of each edge of quilt top. Mark the center of each border.
2. Measure **width** through middle of Quilt Top Center and trim top and bottom borders to determined measurement. To sew borders to quilt top, match center marks and corners, then ease in any fullness (**Fig. 29**).

Fig. 29

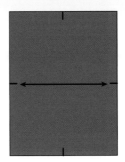

3. Measure **length** through middle of Quilt Top Center including top and bottom borders; trim side borders to determined measurement. Sew side outer borders to Quilt Top Center (**Fig. 30**).

Fig. 30

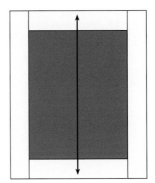

ADDING BORDERS WITH CORNER SQUARES

1. Follow Steps 1 and 2 of **Adding Squared Borders**, page 71.
2. Excluding top/bottom outer borders, measure **length** through middle of Quilt Top Center and add ½" for seam allowances; trim side borders to determined measurement. Sew 1 corner square to each end of side borders; sew side borders to Quilt Top Center (**Fig. 31**).

Fig. 31

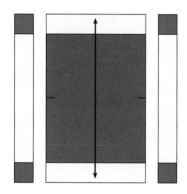

QUILTING

*Quilting holds the three layers (top, batting, and backing) of the quilt together and can be done by hand or machine. All of the projects in this book are machine quilted. Because marking, layering, and quilting are interrelated and may be done in different orders depending on circumstances, please read the entire **Quilting** section, pages 72 - 75, before beginning the quilting process on your project.*

TYPES OF QUILTING

In the Ditch Quilting
Quilting along seamlines or along edges of appliquéd pieces is called "in the ditch" quilting (**Fig. 32**). This type of quilting should be done on the side opposite the seam allowance.

Fig. 32

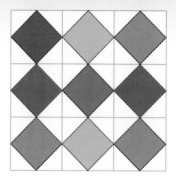

Meandering Quilting
Quilting in random curved lines and swirls is called "meandering" quilting. Quilting lines should not cross or touch each other (**Fig. 33**).

Fig. 33

Motif Quilting

Quilting a design, such as a feathered wreath, is called "motif" quilting ((**Fig. 34**). This type of quilting can be marked before basting quilt layers together.

Fig. 34

Outline Quilting

Quilting approximately ¼" from a seam or appliqué is called "outline" quilting (**Fig. 35**). Outline quilting may be marked, or you may place ¼"w masking tape along seamlines and quilt along the opposite edge of the tape. (Do not leave tape on quilt longer than necessary, since it may leave an adhesive residue.)

Fig. 35

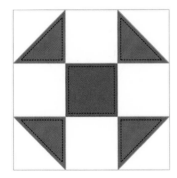

Stipple Quilting

Meandering quilting that is very closely spaced is called "stipple" quilting. Stippling will flatten the area quilted and is often stitched in background areas so that appliquéd or pieced designs will look raised (**Fig. 36**).

Fig. 36

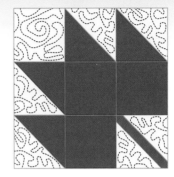

MARKING QUILTING LINES

Quilting lines may be marked using fabric marking pencils, chalk markers, water- or air-soluble pens, or lead pencils.

Simple quilting designs may be marked with chalk or chalk pencil after basting. A small area may be marked, then quilted, before moving to next area to be marked. Intricate designs should be marked before basting using a more durable marker.

Caution: Some marks may be permanently set by pressing. **Test** different markers **on scrap fabric** to find one that marks clearly and can be thoroughly removed.

A wide variety of pre-cut quilting stencils, as well as entire books of quilting patterns, are available. Using a stencil makes it easier to mark intricate or repetitive designs.

CHOOSING AND PREPARING THE BACKING

To allow for slight shifting of the quilt top during quilting, the backing should be approximately 4" larger on all sides than quilt top for bed-sized quilts and large wall hangings and 2" larger for small wall hangings. Yardage requirements listed for quilt backings are calculated for 43/44"w fabric. If it is necessary to piece the backing, use the following instructions.

1. Measure length and width of quilt top; add 8" (4").
2. Cut backing fabric into 2 lengths slightly longer than the determined length measurement. Trim selvages. Place lengths with right sides facing and sew long edges together, forming a tube (**Fig. 37**). Match seams and press along one fold (**Fig. 38**). Cut along pressed fold to form a single piece (**Fig. 39**).

Fig. 37	Fig. 38	Fig. 39

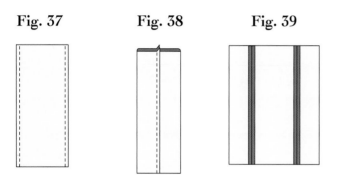

3. Trim backing to correct size, if necessary, and press seam allowances open.

CHOOSING AND PREPARING THE BATTING

Choosing the right batting will make your quilting job easier. The projects in this book are made using cotton batting which does not require tight quilting. If machine quilting, choose a low-loft all cotton or a cotton/polyester blend batting because the cotton helps "grip" the layers of the quilt. For hand quilting, choose a low-loft batting in any of the fiber types described here.

Batting options include cotton/polyester batting, which combines the best of both polyester and cotton battings; fusible battings which do not need to be basted before quilting; bonded polyester which is treated with a protective coating to stabilize the fibers and to reduce "bearding," a process in which batting fibers work their way out through the quilt fabrics; and wool and silk battings, which are generally more expensive and usually only dry-cleanable.

Whichever batting you choose, read the manufacturer's instructions closely for any special notes on care or preparation. When you're ready to use your chosen batting in a project, cut batting the same size as the prepared backing.

ASSEMBLING THE QUILT

1. Examine wrong side of quilt top closely; trim any seam allowances and clip any threads that may show through the front of the quilt. Press quilt top.
2. If quilt top is to be marked before layering, mark quilting lines (see **Marking Quilting Lines**, page 73).
3. Place backing wrong side up on a flat surface. Use masking tape or clamps to adhere edges of backing to surface. Place batting on top of backing fabric. Gently smooth batting, being careful not to stretch or tear. Center quilt top right side up on batting.
4. When machine quilting, use 1" rustproof safety pins to "pin-baste" all layers together, spacing pins approximately 4" apart. Begin at the center and work toward the outer edges to secure all layers. If possible, place pins away from areas that will be quilted, although pins may be removed as needed when quilting.

STRAIGHT-LINE MACHINE QUILTING

The following instructions are for straight-line quilting, which requires a walking foot or even-feed foot. The term "straight-line" is somewhat deceptive, since curves (especially gentle ones) as well as straight lines can be stitched with this technique.

1. Using the same color general-purpose thread in the needle and bobbin avoids "dots" of bobbin thread being pulled to the surface.

2. Using general-purpose thread, which matches the backing in the bobbin, will add pattern and dimension to the quilt back without adding contrasting color. Refer to your owner's manual for recommended tension settings.

3. Set the stitch length for 6 - 10 stitches per inch and attach the walking foot to sewing machine.

4. After pin-basting, decide which section of the quilt will have the longest continuous quilting line, oftentimes the area from center top to center bottom. Leaving the area exposed where you will place your first line of quilting, roll up each edge of the quilt to help reduce the bulk, keeping fabrics smooth. Smaller projects may not need to be rolled.

5. Start stitching at beginning of longest quilting line, using very short stitches for the first ¼" to "lock" beginning of quilting line. Stitch across project, using one hand on each side of the walking foot to slightly spread the fabric and to guide the fabric through the machine. Lock stitches at end of quilting line.

6. Continue machine quilting, stitching longer quilting lines first to stabilize the quilt before moving on to other areas.

FREE-MOTION MACHINE QUILTING

Free-motion quilting may be free form or may follow a marked quilting pattern.

1. Using the same color general-purpose thread in the needle and bobbin avoids "dots" of bobbin thread being pulled to the surface. Use general-purpose thread in the bobbin and decorative thread for stitching, such as metallic, variegated or contrasting-colored general-purpose thread, when you desire the quilting to be more pronounced.

2. Use a darning foot and drop or cover feed dogs. Pull up bobbin thread and hold both thread ends while you stitch 2 or 3 stitches in place to lock thread. Cut threads near quilt surface.

3. Place hands lightly on quilt on either side of darning foot to slightly spread fabric and to move fabric through the machine. Even stitch length is achieved by using smooth, flowing hand motion and steady machine speed. Slow machine speed and fast hand movement will create long stitches. Fast machine speed and slow hand movement will create short stitches. Move quilt sideways, back and forth in a circular motion, or in a random motion to create the desired designs; do not rotate quilt. Lock stitches at the end of each quilting line.

MAKING A HANGING SLEEVE

Attaching a hanging sleeve to the back of your wall hanging or quilt before the binding is added allows you to display your completed project on a wall.

1. Press short edges of fabric piece ¼" to wrong side; press edges ¼" to wrong side again and machine stitch in place.

2. Matching wrong sides, fold piece in half lengthwise to form a tube.

3. Follow project instructions to sew binding to quilt top and to trim backing and batting. Before blind stitching binding to backing, match raw edges and stitch hanging sleeve to center top edge on back of wall hanging.

4. Finish binding wall hanging, treating the hanging sleeve as part of the backing.

5. Blind stitch bottom of hanging sleeve to backing, taking care not to stitch through to front of quilt.

6. Insert dowel or slat into hanging sleeve.

BINDING

MAKING STRAIGHT-GRAIN BINDING

Binding encloses the raw edges of the quilt. Binding strips may be cut from the straight lengthwise or crosswise grain of the fabric. Straight-grain binding works well for projects with straight edges, for small projects, and to accentuate fabric designs such as stripes.

1. Cut crosswise or lengthwise strips of binding fabric the width and length called for in the project instructions. With right sides together, sew the short ends of the strips together to achieve the necessary length for continuous binding.

2. Press seams allowances open. Press under one long edge of binding ¼" to the wrong side.

ATTACHING BINDING WITH MITERED CORNERS

1. Press 1 end of binding diagonally (**Fig. 40**).

Fig. 40

2. Beginning with pressed end several inches from a corner, lay binding around project to make sure that seams in binding will not end up at a corner. Adjust placement if necessary. Matching raw edge(s) of binding to raw edge of project top, pin binding to right side of project along one edge.

3. When you reach the first corner, mark ¼" from corner of project top (**Fig. 41**).

Fig. 41

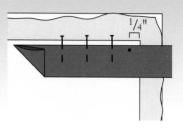

4. Using a ¼" seam allowance, sew binding to project, backstitching at beginning of stitching and when you reach the mark (**Fig. 42**). Lift needle out of fabric and clip thread.

Fig. 42

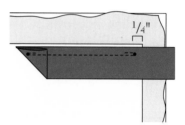

5. Fold binding as shown in **Figs. 43** and **44** and pin binding to adjacent side, matching raw edges When you reach the next corner, mark ¼" from edge of project top.

Fig. 43   **Fig. 44**

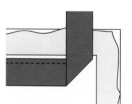 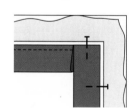

5. Backstitching at edge of project top, sew pinned binding to quilt (**Fig. 45**); backstitch when you reach the next mark. Lift needle out of fabric and clip thread.

Fig. 45

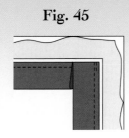

7. Repeat Steps 5 and 6 to continue sewing binding to project until binding overlaps beginning end by approximately 2". Trim excess binding.
8. Trim backing and batting even with edges of project top.
9. On one edge of project, fold binding over to project backing and pin pressed edge in place, covering stitching line (**Fig. 46**). On adjacent side, fold binding over, forming a mitered corner (**Fig. 47**). Repeat to pin remainder of binding in place.

Fig. 46   **Fig. 47**

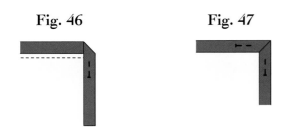

10. Blindstitch binding to backing, taking care not to stitch through to front of project. Following **Fig. 48**, come up at **1**, go down at **2**, and come up at **3**. Length of stitches may be varied.

Fig. 48

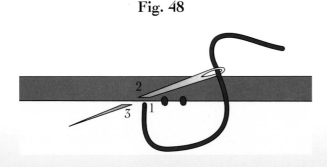

ATTACHING BINDING WITH OVERLAPPED CORNERS

1. Matching raw edges and using ¹/₄" seam allowance, sew a length of binding to top and bottom edges on right side of quilt.
2. Trim backing and batting even with edges of quilt top.
3. Trim ends of top and bottom binding even with edges of quilt top. Fold binding over to quilt backing and pin pressed edges in place, covering stitching line (**Fig. 49**); blindstitch binding to backing.

Fig. 49

4. Leaving approximately 1¹/₂" of binding at each end, stitch a length of binding to each side edge of quilt. Trim backing and batting as in Step 2.
5. Trim each end of binding ¹/₂" longer than bound edge. Fold each end of binding over to quilt backing (**Fig. 50**); pin in place. Fold binding over to quilt backing and blindstitch in place, taking care not to stitch through to front of quilt.

Fig. 50

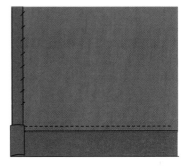

PAT'S MACHINE-SEWN BINDING

For a quick and easy finish when attaching straight-grain binding with overlapped corners, Pat sews her binding to the back of the quilt and topstitches it in place on the front, eliminating all hand stitching.

Fig. 52

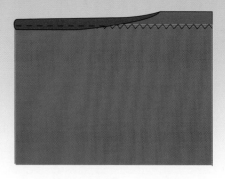

1. Using a narrow zigzag, stitch around quilt close to the raw edges (**Fig. 51**). Trim backing and batting even with edges of quilt top.

Fig. 51

4. Leaving approximately $1\frac{1}{2}$" of binding at each end, stitch a length of binding to wrong side of each side of quilt.

5. Trim each end of binding $\frac{1}{2}$" longer than bound edge. Fold under each raw end of binding. (**Fig. 53**); pin in place. Fold binding over to quilt front and topstitch in place, as in Step 3.

2. Matching raw edges and using $\frac{1}{4}$" seam allowance, sew a length of binding to top and bottom edges on wrong side of quilt.

3. Fold binding over to quilt front and pin pressed edges in place, covering stitching line (**Fig. 52**); Topstitch binding close to pressed edge. Trim ends of top and bottom binding even with edges of quilt top.

Fig. 53

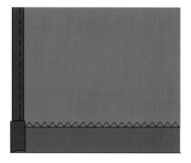

Metric Conversion Chart

Inches x 2.54 = centimeters (cm)   Yards x .9144 = meters (m)
Inches x 25.4 = millimeters (mm)   Yards x 91.44 = centimeters (cm)
Inches x .0254 = meters (m)   Centimeters x .3937 = inches (")
                                     Meters x 1.0936 = yards (yd)

Standard Equivalents

$1/8$"	3.2 mm	0.32 cm	$1/8$ yard	11.43 cm	0.11 m
$1/4$"	6.35 mm	0.635 cm	$1/4$ yard	22.86 cm	0.23 m
$3/8$"	9.5 mm	0.95 cm	$3/8$ yard	34.29 cm	0.34 m
$1/2$"	12.7 mm	1.27 cm	$1/2$ yard	45.72 cm	0.46 m
$5/8$"	15.9 mm	1.59 cm	$5/8$ yard	57.15 cm	0.57 m
$3/4$"	19.1 mm	1.91 cm	$3/4$ yard	68.58 cm	0.69 m
$7/8$"	22.2 mm	2.22 cm	$7/8$ yard	80 cm	0.8 m
1"	25.4 mm	2.54 cm	1 yard	91.44 cm	0.91 m

EDITORIAL STAFF

Vice President and Editor-in-Chief:
  Sandra Graham Case
Executive Director of Publications:
  Cheryl Nodine Gunnells
Senior Publications Director: Susan White Sullivan
Director of Designer Relations: Debra Nettles
Publication Operations Director: Cheryl Johnson
Editorial Director: Susan Frantz Wiles
*Senior Director of Public Relations and Retail
  Marketing:* Stephen Wilson
Photography Director: Karen Hall
Senior Art Operations Director: Jeff Curtis

TECHNICAL/EDITORIAL

Technical Editor: Lisa Lancaster
Technical Writer: Jean Lewis
Editorial Associate: Steven M. Cooper

ART

Art Publications Director: Rhonda Shelby
Art Imaging Director: Mark Hawkins
Art Category Manager: Lora Puls
Graphic Artists: Dayle Carozza, Stephanie Hamling,
  and Mandy Hickman
Photostylists: Cassie Newsome
Publishing Systems Administrator: Becky Riddle
Publishing Systems Assistants: Clint Hanson and
  John Rose

BUSINESS STAFF

Publisher: Rick Barton
Vice President, Finance: Tom Siebenmorgen
Director of Corporate Planning and Development:
  Laticia Mull Dittrich
Vice President, Retail Marketing: Bob Humphrey
Vice President, Sales: Ray Shelgosh
Vice President, National Accounts: Pam Stebbins
Director of Sales and Services: Margaret Reinold
Vice President, Operations: Jim Dittrich
Comptroller, Operations: Rob Thieme
Retail Customer Service Manager: Stan Raynor
Print Production Manager: Fred F. Pruss

Other Leisure Arts publications by Pat Sloan:

- Learn to Appliqué with Pat Sloan – Leaflet # 3784
  ISBN 157486-452-1
- Friend-to-Friend Quilts – Leaflet #3681
- I Can't Believe I'm Quilting – Leaflet #3649
- Quilt The Seasons With Pat Sloan – Leaflet #3574
- Vintage Blooms – Leaflet #3558
- Folksy Favorites – Leaflet #3391
  ISBN 1-57486-327-4

Made in the United States of America

ISBN 1-57486-447-5

10 9 8 7 6 5 4 3 2 1